With this book...

- You'll be able to grow your business in some amazing new ways.

- Communicate your powerful vision across the business.

- Gain clarity on your true purpose and values.

- Drive your core strategies in the Long, Medium and Short Term

- Understand the Key Actions you need to take this month

- Orchestrate Rhythm and Pulse throughout the business

- Create Legend and get everyone fully aligned

  BUT ONLY if you use this book to take ACTION.
  This book is not for Shelf-Development

Deri

Who is this book for?

This book is intended for Business Leaders, all of whom will be SMEs (or Small to Medium Enterprise in non-jargon speak), so let us define what that means, as this is another misunderstood term.

SMEs go up to £250 million – in my world that isn't small or medium! But to make this as inclusive and focused as possible, let's settle on a definition of a business from start-up to a modest £10 million. I hope that includes you.

Once you grow to over £10 million, these principles still apply, but you may need multiple pages and divisional pages in order to make this work effectively and cascade it through your organization.

There is no doubt though that the quickest way to reach a £10 million turnover is to put all the following principles into action. So if you are up for that, then it is time to sharpen your pencil.

"Complexity is your enemy. Any fool can make something complicated. It is hard to make something simple."

Richard Branson

What people are saying

A powerful management tool to help the board stay on track and focused on the *"real" tasks that add value and deliver results. I would gladly recommend Deri to* any entrepreneur, business owner or board member looking to take their organisation to the next level.
Jason Roos Direct Response

Deri's like our Business TOMTOM. We told him our goal and he's mapped out a clear route of how to get there in the quickest, easiest possible way.
Jeff Spires Pow New Media

Working with Deri is a real privilege and his advice has already yielded tangible internal and external results within our organisation. His business acumen is clearly second to none and is combined with an extremely approachable and personable outlook. I cannot recommend Deri and BGI highly enough.
Jeremy Newton TradeDoubler

I have no hesitation in recommending Deri if you wish to keep Strategy simple but effective and incorporating accountability.
Peter J Lynagh Academy of Chief Executives

Having worked with Deri for over a year now, his sessions have helped us come up with a clear strategy, move away from a business that was going nowhere, make difficult decisions & lead us to a much better place.

Knowing Deri has been through just about every situation we are likely to encounter means we know he can offer no-nonsense advice to help us grow our business.

The one-pager concept is our central reference point, a business plan on a page & having accountability is a key part. In short, Deri is great & we hope to work with him for many years.

Mark Wallis, The Number Nerds

What is Strategy on a Page ™ all about?

Most companies are unclear on their strategy and lack a proven method for recording their actions or holding themselves accountable.

Ask yourself the following questions:

- Are you 100% clear on what your targets are this month in the five main areas of your business, and who is responsible for the actions?

- Do you trust yourself and hold yourself accountable to meet your targets?

- Have you forecasted the impact of meeting those targets over the next few months?

- The methodology and framework are based around Strategy on a Page™, which is STRATEGY from PURPOSE all the way through to accountability & monthly action on one single page of A4.

Strategy on a Page™ came from Deri's extensive business experience and MBA through advising over 125 companies and experience on his MBA, angel and venture capital networks. It has been proven to work with one-person companies to 500 million pound companies. It's not been worked on a billion-dollar company yet.

The one-page plan was created when Deri was asked on numerous occasions in investment proposals and raising capital: what was the essence of the business? This is normally illustrated with an Executive Plan, but many templates don't work as businesses are unique. Additionally, by the time they are written, they are out of date because strategy and the world move so fast.

Therefore, Strategy on a Page™ combats the speed and acceleration in the business world by enabling us to strategically adapt to the changes in external and internal markets. The concept provides a monthly accountability system, being able to flex strategy in the now, medium term and long term.

This methodology doesn't come lightly – it has taken him 17 years to get strategy on one single page, and it's very powerful and unique..

"If you do not plan to succeed, by default, you are planning to fail"

Deri ap John Llewellyn Davies

When it comes to Deri Llewellyn-Davies, there aren't many men out there who spend their days in a boardroom and their spare time climbing the highest summits in the world. Deri loves business and adventure in equal measure and his same motivation underpins both: a fascination with life and a curiosity that always leads him to ask, "Why?"

That questioning is key in his role as CEO of Business Growth International, as he helps leaders in both FTSE 500 and entrepreneurial companies to take their businesses (and themselves) to the next level. With over 28 years' experience of the commercial markets, Deri knows that whatever issues his clients are facing – from funding shortages to management fall outs, corporate redundancy to bankruptcy – he's personally been there and got the T-shirt.

It's exactly that experience which fuels his ability to look at their business and connect the hidden dots, to lead him to the heart of the issue. But the real value comes with Deri's straight-talking truthfulness, which means he puts all the cards on the table, creates a proactive plan of action and holds people accountable so it happens. It gets results: on one occasion he was brought in to prepare a failing company for sale but instead turned it around and within six months took its profits from the red into the black. This is why he is sought out as a NED and strategic advisor.

Deri still makes time for his adventures though, and is part of the way through a self-styled 'Global Adventurer's Grand Slam' – something he came up with aged 30, when an injury gained during an international tournament ended his rugby career.

Having completed the Marathon des Sables (the toughest thing he says he'll ever do) and climbed five of the world's highest summits, Deri has only two more mountains, both Poles, and a jungle marathon to go…though the biggest challenge will be convincing his wife and children!

Dedication

This book is dedicated to my family.

Strategy is all about doing what you
love, serving others in the process,
adding huge value and capitalising on opportunity.
If we are successful in this, we earn more than enough
money to live the lifestyle we choose.

My ultimate lifestyle is driven by my time in my
beautiful country home with my beautiful family.

Hayley, my soul mate and love of my life,
who keeps me grounded,
Aarrowen Devine, the one most like me,
Eliona Seren, the organiser
Maddisynne Mai, the cuddler

Loghan ap Deri my little warrior

I love you all more than words can say.

The Page

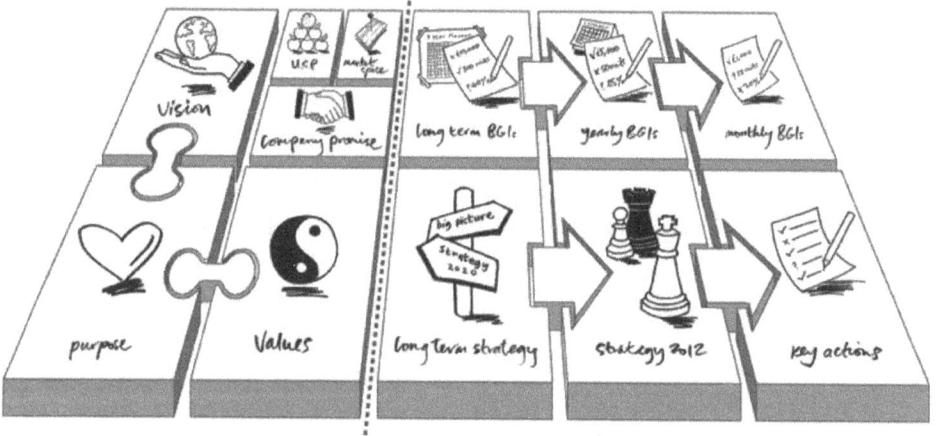

Volume One

STRATEGY on a page

THE MYTHS AND LEGENDS

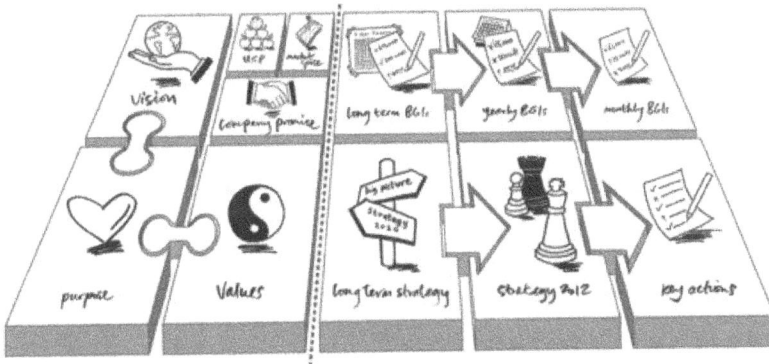

The new strategy tool for the new world of business

Deri ap John Llewellyn Davies

Published by

Filament Publishing Ltd
14, Croydon Road, Beddington,
Croydon, Surrey, CR0 4PA

Telephone 020 8688 2598

email: info@filamentpublishing.com
www.filamentpublishing.com

ISBN 978-1-915465-51-1

Printed in the UK

Table of Contents

"The journey of
a thousand leagues
begins with a
single step."

Lao Tzu
531 BC

Foreword

This book is my life's work. It is all the lessons in business I have accumulated over the years, what made some businesses work and others not, all the lessons from my mentors and all the lessons from the tens of thousands of pounds worth of personal and professional development over the years. It's the first book in a series. But the keystone.

This is a book to be experienced, to be discovered not just as a boring strategy textbook that sits on the shelf. As such, it needed to be brought alive. This wouldn't have been possible without the amazing work from Chris Day of Filament Publishing, who has shaped this book and added the creative brilliance you will see throughout. He also enabled the message to be understood by all when I was overcomplicating things or couldn't see why some things weren't obvious. Chris, you are a genius! (Quite literally too!) Also, the original support and guidance of Kelly Dunworth, whose experience and creative input has taken the book to a new level and guided the ultimate theme.

A huge thank you to all my clients who stories are dotted throughout the book, and my mentors for guiding me.

But most of all, I want to thank you, the reader, for having the guts to pick up this book and immerse yourself in strategy. I honour your entrepreneurial spirit and your drive.

This book will serve you, if you will let it, so let's get on with the adventure...

C ome on in, you are welcome! Now, we've probably never met, but the chances are that if you have chosen to read this book, then there is a high probability that you are either the owner of a business, or in a senior management position within your organisation.

You're probably busy, so I won't waste your time with a fluffy introduction. Let's get straight to business. I am known in real life consulting as the straight-talking strategy guy – and this book is intended to reflect this.

If you are expecting a highly theoretical strategy book full of complex theories and algorithms, you are better off elsewhere as this book is simple, practical and powerful. If you are seeking some jargon and buzz words to bounce around the office and impress your friends, you are also sadly in the wrong place, as this is a book about doing, about accountability and about alignment.

However, if you are seeking a real tool, proven by countless businesses to make a dramatic difference; a tool that is simple, powerful and effective; a tool that holds you accountable to the very purpose behind your company every day, then you are in the right place.

By the end of this book, not only will you fully understand how to use it but, if you follow the chapters and exercises, you will wonder how you ever managed without it!

Introduction to Strategy

For me, a good and effective strategy is the foundation of any successful enterprise, big or small. Get this bit right, and everything else logically follows on. There is only one thing that comes before strategy and that is purpose, but more on that later.

Of course, there is many a learned tome on the subject. Over the years, some highly intelligent and experienced business leaders have felt moved to transfer a lifetime's worth of knowledge on the subject into five or six hundred closely worded pages. Indeed, some of these books are very good and I have read my fair share through my own business education and MBA. But not many are accessible to the SME and produce a practical tool that you can do something with now.

However, you may have noticed that this book does not fit this description. **Strategy on a Page**™ is deliberately compact, and it also contains a lot of space. This is for a very good reason.

If you are at the coalface of your business and juggling all the day-to-day challenges and opportunities that life throws at you, even the thought of picking up a 500 page book on strategy might be a step too far, let alone finding the time to read it. I was therefore determined to write a book that didn't come into the category of "Shelf Development" and sit on a shelf, never to be opened. Instead, I have designed this to be accessible, easy to use and quick to implement. I want you to get quick results and some early wins, whilst building a long term tool of accountability.

However, I recognise that by reading this book you could be at any one of a number of points on your own journey, from being at the pre start-up phase of your business, to being Chairman of the Board of a global business. I have therefore designed this book to be a window onto the subject, to help you to access those parts of this process that are relevant to your needs right now, in the fastest possible way.

Next, I signpost you to more detailed tools and resources for you to access as needed. One of these is the Strategy Online toolkit.

Now I won't go into much detail about this yet because that would be putting the cart before the horse. However, once you have worked your way through the book and completed your Page, you will fully understand the value of this incredible tool and how it will hold you accountable on a month by month basis. More about it later on.

But understanding what strategy is (and isn't) and how to formulate it, is not just for Christmas, or for the next presentation you have to make to the board, your shareholders, or even your wife, but it is a skill that will help you in every area of your life. Believe me, I know.

Strategy on a Page™ is exactly what it says on the tin.
One simple page that can make one massive difference to you and your business.

When I am not working with business leaders and helping to take their businesses (and themselves) to the next level, my hobby is climbing mountains and other extreme sports. For example, I have completed the notorious Marathon des Sables across the Sahara Desert (the toughest thing I've ever done!) and climbed five of the world's highest summits.

I only mention this to demonstrate that I have used my **Strategy on a Page**™ principles in all of these cases. If they can take me successfully to the top of some of the highest mountains in the world and safely across the desert, then I believe they are robust enough to take you and your business to wherever you want to go.

For more on my adventurous side, read my book "Life's Great Adventure", which gives you the life tools to complement the business tools in this book. All author royalties go to charity, so you will be doing good whilst getting inspired! What a potent mix.

So just before we start, one word about this book. The late Mortimer Adler, a past editor of Encyclopaedia Britannica, wrote a book called "How to Read a Book". In it he encourages the reader to make notes in the margin; underline or highlight helpful passages; draw diagrams, and indeed anything else that helps to bring the content in the book to life and to make it memorable. I encourage you to do the same. This is not intended to be a work of reference, but instead a tool to help you make a difference, and help you and your business on your journey to the next level.

As such, we have purposefully left space in the sections to make notes and start to get your **Strategy on a Page** ™.

But most importantly, this book is about giving you the knowledge and tools to take action. Action is the key to making this stuff work.

Never forget, "To know and not to do is not to know". Time to get started.

Without continual growth and progress, such words as improvement, achievement, and success have no meaning.

Benjamin Franklin

Chapter One

Definitions

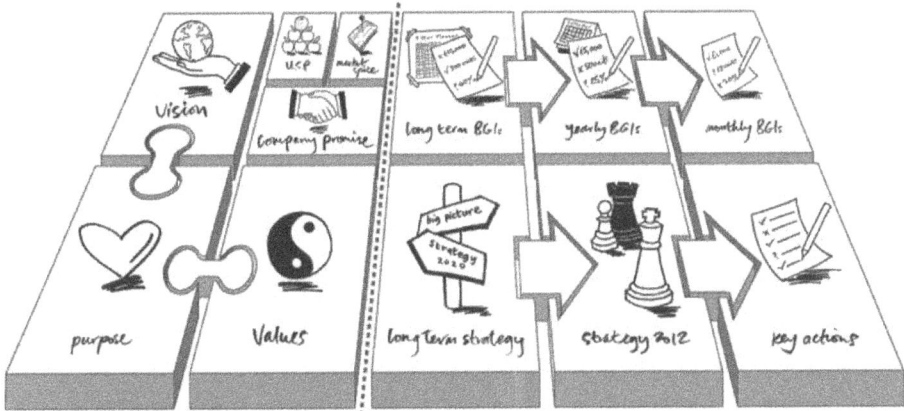

ight up front, I am going to promise you that this is going to be a jargon-free zone. You won't find any clever acronyms or magic formulas, just tried and tested common sense which has been further tested by the many businesses which I have had the privilege to work with over the years. I will use some of their stories and experiences so you can see how all this stuff works in the real world, frankly the only one that is worth inhabiting.

So, what is strategy?

If you have ever attended one of my CEO forums, Congresses or Keynotes, this is one of the first questions I ask, "What is strategy?" .... So before we move on, I want you to consider this question from your perspective.... What is strategy?

What does it mean to you? Take a moment to think and write down your answer in the space provided.

I conclude that strategy is like three blind men trying to describe an elephant! I use this example as a way of illustrating why it is that many of us have differing views as to what strategy really is.

Picture an elephant in the room and our three blindfolded volunteers each only able to feel a part of the animal. One can only feel the tail, the other, its trunk, and the third, a leg.

From this limited amount of information, each one of them tries to describe the whole animal.

The man at the tail thinks it is like a string and a pom- pom, the man at the foot thinks it is like a tree and the man at the trunk thinks it is like a snake.

Not an easy task and one that is further clouded by their perception, their point of view and their mindset. Do try this at home with your own elephant if you don't believe me! When you only have a part of the picture, it is almost impossible. The point being that strategy is the whole elephant!

A clear definition

L et's get a clear definition of strategy for the purpose of this book; outside you can use whatever you want. The dictionary definition describes it as "a plan for obtaining a specific major result". This is different to the dictionary definition of a tactic which is defined as "a plan for promoting desired end results".

So no wonder strategy and tactics are kind of mixed up quite a lot because they've got very similar meanings. There is, however, one subtle difference and it is one word "MAJOR". When I'm talking about strategy, I'm talking about major results.

It's going to make a major difference to your business, not tinkering around or tweaking it. So, when we're talking about strategy, think about major results in your business, something that's going to give you a shift change, a quantum change. That's what I mean by strategy.

Now this is where it's getting interesting and specific to you, as what is major to a large corporation (where most books on strategy are born) is not major to a small company. I don't care what major looks like as long as it is major to you!

One other note on strategy that we have eluded to and that is the role of perception. Depending on your background and skills, you will view strategy differently. Again, in my speaking engagements I ask the question, "Who is from a sales and marketing background?" And usually half the room's hands go up. I then follow up with, "Keep your hands up if you have a clear and robust financial strategy and are good with the numbers in your business," and I then get a plummeting of hands.

I do this vice versa with financial and operations, and ask how their creative and innovation strategy is. This is consistent and insightful. Depending on our backgrounds, we will be biased in our approach to strategy. So what is your bias? And what is your weakness? We will come back to this later…

I do know that you would not be reading this book if you were not already a long way down your own journey as a business leader, or indeed more than well qualified to be setting up your own new enterprise, so I will not insult your intelligence by being over simplistic.

However, on my own journey, working with literally hundreds of business of all sizes, I have found that there are so many different interpretations as to what strategy really is that I found myself talking more about this than anything else. That is why this book had to be written.

Keeping it simple

So many aspects of business are made far more complicated than they need to be. This certainly applies to strategy.

I am a fervent believer that if something cannot be adequately described on a single sheet of paper, then it is too complicated. I therefore set myself the challenge of creating **Strategy on a Page** to prove this point.

I have now used and tested this simple process so many times that I know it works. If you put it into action, I know that you will gain the clarity it can give to help you achieve the business and personal goals you aspire to. In my humble opinion, if you can't get your entire strategy on a page from your macro-purpose all the way down what you are doing today, then it could be that you are trying too hard. It may be a lot less complicated than you think.

I have learnt that there are two ways to do everything: the wrong way and the way your wife told you! With strategy in a business, I believe there is simply Good Strategy and Bad Strategy. So, how can you tell the difference?

If you have ever driven through Slough (a town in the uk), you will know that there is a long stretch of road with traffic lights at regular intervals. They are timed in such a way as to allow you to flow straight through on a green light the entire length of the road, providing you stick exactly to the speed limit. If you try to rush, you end up stopping at each one. Very clever!

Now, a Good Strategy is like that. Get it right, and your business surges smoothly ahead.

Get it wrong and it is stop/start all the way. And that's how you can stall.

I was first introduced to the concept of **Strategy on a Page** by the confectionery giant, Mars, where a part of my early career was spent. They are an amazing organisation in many ways and they had this down to a fine art. At that time, they were using huge sheets of A3 with tiny 8 point type to contain all the information on. Not the easiest to read, but it started me thinking on this journey to make it simple.

I am very fortunate to have travelled extensively around the world in business, which has given me the opportunity to stay at the cutting edge of all this stuff. The Harvard Business Review, McKinsey, Gazelles and the Rockefeller Habits, for example, all have some really cool insights and this area of strategy is ever evolving. But, if you don't have time to explore then don't panic, I have done it for you and distilled 17 years of work, education and exploration into this one page concept.

When I did part of my MBA over in The Anderson School, UCLA California, I was on the venture capital circuit (The Global Access Program), which put me in front of many people who had written a business plan and tried to raise money on the back of it.

Those people who managed to succinctly describe their project on a single page, or in a single model, were the ones who succeeded in getting the attention of the Business Angels and VCs. Another lesson to be learnt.

For anyone who has written a business plan or indeed read one, I ask you, what is the most important page?.... Page 1 of course, so why not get the whole plan distilled onto one page....

More on this next chapter.

The Myths and Legends
of Strategy

Myth One

Strategy is only really necessary if you are a huge multinational. SMEs and the rest of us can get by with a few scribbled notes on the back of a fag packet and a long to-do list to tick off. Wrong! A list of 112 action points doesn't mean you have a strategy. Just a list! And this list will never end…bummer!

Myth Two

Another myth about strategy is that it's expensive, and it's time consuming. In business circles there are many jokes about how "consultants" get brought into a company to help formulate strategy and justify their exorbitant fees by creating large unintelligible PowerPoint presentations and business plans that sit in the drawer gathering dust after they have left. And, sadly, consultants are used sometimes to justify an internal decision and to pass blame if it goes pear shaped.

There is considerable arse-covering going on out there. Shame on them, I say!

The truth is that strategy doesn't have to be expensive. With the right education and the right focus, it can be totally free. Every business leader should have the basic skills and strategy to be able to map their own.

Alternatively, it's my belief that, in my own consultancy the strategy element with any client should be very quick, powerful and to the point. I very rarely spend more than two hours a month with my clients. They don't need any more time from me for that, which makes strategy for SMEs very affordable if it's focused.

Myth Three

Strategy takes too much time. No matter what size your business and how many or few people you have to delegate to, there never seems enough time to do everything. Strategy is often put off because the myth is that it takes a lot of time. You and I know that you can succeed in any business by just working half days. It doesn't matter which 12 hours you choose.

But, seriously, if you are so busy fire fighting and doing the day-to-day, and are not finding time to do the basics, the question is, are you really doing the right things? The whole Ready – Aim – Fire scenario. It doesn't take that long to line up the right shot before you pull the trigger, strategy is the "aim" bit, I suggest you do it first before you kill the wrong thing. Maybe even you...

Myth Four

Another myth is that having a Business Plan covers strategy. Certainly a Business Plan is aligned to the definition of strategy which, as you remember is "a plan to obtain a major result." (Just making sure you were paying attention!)

The problem is that a lot of people have a bad experience or a bad feeling around The Business Plan. A bit like Marmite, you either love it or loathe it.

If you have been through the long and arduous process of creating a comprehensive business plan to then see it ignored, it does colour your judgement as to whether you should put yourself though a seemingly pointless exercise again, or just get on with running the business.

I'd like to pose a question. Do you have a business plan, or have you ever written one? If not, why not? If so, where is it right now and are you actively using it to guide the strategic direction of your company?

From those whom I speak to in CEO and business leader groups, 80% of them have at some point written a plan but have then not used it. I find that most who give me an honest answer will admit that their plans are sitting in the drawer, hard drive of their computer or filing cabinet. What a waste!

The amazing thing when it is fished out of a drawer and they actually flick through it, there's often a lot of really good value points. If they'd actually done half of what they said they were going to do, the company would probably be in a very different shape.

Therefore, although business plans have their place and they are actually important, particularly for raising capital, they do not bridge the gap between what is strategy and actually holding yourself accountable month in month out to the major strategic objectives of the company.

The big problem with Business Plans is the moment they are finished, they are out of date. So we need a better tool.

Myth Five

Still on the subject of myths, have you ever been on one of those Blue Sky Thinking days. They usually take place in a country hotel and you are locked into a hot room on the only sunny day that year and are not allowed to leave until you have collectively come up with a series of improbable ideas. The danger is that what comes out of these events is often mistaken for strategy.

Myth Six

Sorry, but "Fluff" is not acceptable. By Fluff, I mean restating the obvious, masquerading as expertise. Recently I heard of a strategy from a seriously large global organisation. I won't name and shame them, but I will say that they were in the financial sector (Source McKinsey: Bad Strategy)

Their primary strategy was quoted to me as "customer- centric financial growth". All they were actually saying was, "We focus on the customer, and help them to grow financially." Well of course they did, they were a bank. So basically their strategy was, "We are a bank."

That's what I mean by Fluff. It means nothing, but it sounds quite sophisticated. Don't be fooled, it is not strategy.

Myth Seven

Goals are not strategy

One of the most common myths I encounter in guise of strategy is goals. When I ask audiences, "Who has a strategy and who is brave enough to define it?" I usually get one or two confident brave souls whose hands thrust into the air (bearing in mind by this point I have defined what strategy is). I ask them to define their strategy and I have a variety of answers, the most common one being, "To be a £X million business by the end of the year," replace X with whatever figure you like and million with thousand if needs be but the answers are all similar. To which I respond, "That is a GOAL, not a strategy." So don't confuse them. When I then probe further to what is the plan behind the goal and its different facets, the confidence evaporates and the stuttering begins, there usually is very little strategy behind the goals. That is why very few goals are achieved.

Now, don't get me wrong, goals are very important, but a goal without a strategy is like a car without an engine; it isn't going very far.

Myth Eight

The final myth I'd like to put to bed is the high energy "Motivational Ra! Ra!" that you sometimes come across in the direct sales world. To us Brits, it comes across as a bit American. It's the kind of, let's just win, yeah, let's go, go get 'em, oooh. How we going to get 'em? No idea! Let's just go anyway, yeah!

So is this strategy? I don't think so. As you may know, I like rugby, and what I like about it is that it's a good game of strategy. If you just go out and shout, "Let's win! Forget about the scrums and line-outs, we're just going to win". It's not going to work.

Those are all my myths or Bad Strategy, if you prefer. Compared with all of that Good Strategy which is a lot simpler. In fact, one of my ways of benchmarking good strategy is that when looked at in retrospect, it is both simple and obvious – and doesn't need a lot of jargon or management-speak to dress it up.

If it is simple, it will get done. If it is complicated and difficult, it won't – and will lie in the drawer adding nothing to the business. Let me explain how important this is.

As we each year goes by, we find the world has changed. There is no point in going back to what worked before. That was yesterday, and it is gone. The world now is a lot faster and many business leaders are caught in the headlights not knowing which way to jump. A recent survey highlighted the fact that many leaders are just not adequately prepared for the future.

If the role of a leader is, as the name suggests, to lead people, it is also to drive strategic planning, inspiring commitment and managing change. Most people are poor at those skills. In study after study, the one thing that business leaders are the worst at is strategy! It's more than a bit worrying considering that most of the people in these surveys were MBAs! So what chance does the poor SME have.

Lack of alignment

Harris Interactive, a research organisation, recently did a study of 23,000 workers. They found that around 80% did not understand how their jobs relate to their company's organisational goals. So that is 80% of the workforce who don't have any clue what their job's all about!

Now that might have worked in the past, that might have worked in the last generation, but it will not work in the generation we're moving into. It won't work in my generation and it certainly won't work in the generations below me. Because the next generation wants to feel they're aligned to something. They want to feel like their company believes in something and it's not happening.

The survey went on to identify that 70% of employees say managers don't provide clear goals and directions. When they delved deeper, the reason was because most of those managers didn't know what goals to provide because they didn't have them themselves.

That was simply because they didn't have a clear strategy.

This is where strategy links to goals. Of course, goals are important but they are only meaningful if there is a strategy in place and ultimate goals for the organisation to hang them from.

So, now we know what strategy is, and what it isn't. We also know why it is so important to a business and why it is important to you.

Now let's move to the next stage, creating your own Strategy on a Page. Let's get going!

Key points

Strategy is a plan for obtaining a major specific result

- Strategy should be simple and cost effective
- Having your business plan on one page of A4 is critical when raising finance
- Strategic planning doesn't have to be time consuming, as long as you put in a regular rhythm

Goals are not strategy. They are the outcome of the plan

Introducing 'The Page'

This is a sample of the page you will completing, stage by stage, at the end of each chapter.
Alternatively, this can be completed via the BGI Strategy App - www.BGIStrategyApp.com

Vision - Expression of Purpose	USP	Strategy 5 years 2017	Goals (2012) Business Growth Indicators	Goals (This Month) Business Growth Indicators
1				
2	Defined Market Space			
3				
4	Company Promise			
5				

Purpose - Reason for being	Values/Principles - Stories	Core Strategy - long term	Strategy Driver - Yearly	Key Actions
1	1	1	1	1
2	2	2	2	2
3	3	3	3	3
4	4	4	4	4
5	5	5	5	5

Chapter Two

Preparation

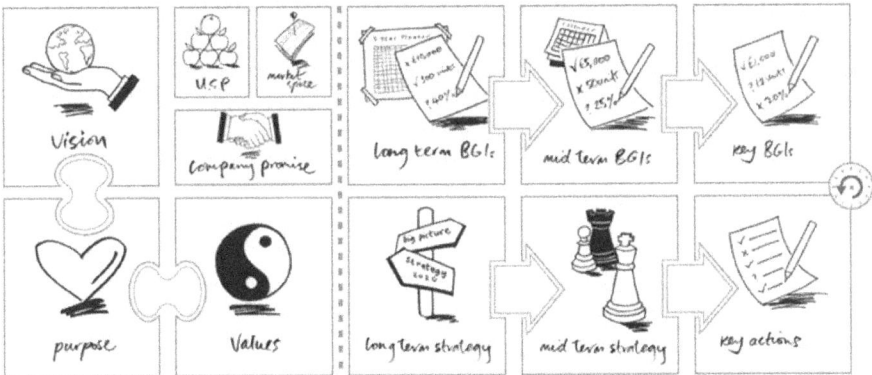

I f you speak to any writer, they will tell you that it is easier to write a thousand words on any given subject than it is to condense that same content down into one hundred. I suppose that is why, when working with businesses, there seems to be a belief that the longer a document is, the more value it contains. In reality, I believe there must be an inverse law somewhere which states that the larger and more unwieldy a document is, the less likely it is to be read and the more likely it will spend its life locked in a dark drawer or in the dark recesses of your computer.

Bigger isn't always better!

As I said in Chapter One, the number of so-called strategy documents I have seen which take thousands of words to say very little, tells me that people just keep on writing in the hope that they might stumble across what it is they want to say. But that mindset stops here! This chapter is all about how to get total clarity on your company strategy, and communicate it on one simple page.

It is no use saying, "Well, we have a big complicated business, so that would be impossible," because I have spent three decades proving the opposite with some of the largest and most successful companies on the planet, as well as many far smaller ones who are successfully moving in that direction.

It can be done, and I will show you how!

In our fast paced world, almost everybody suffers from being time poor. If you are not, then you are probably not in full possession of the facts! For me, that is why getting complicated things like strategy down to a single page was so vital. Everybody has time to read and refer to one page. It can even be pinned to the wall by your desk.

One page is easy to read, easy to understand and easy to put into action, so you will not have any excuses!

Not only that, but the principles apply no matter what size your enterprise may currently have reached.

Also, with the advent of iPads and the like and the prevalence of laptops, you need something you can see on one screen, even as your screen saver, so it's right in front of you at all times, that's where you will find the Strategy toolkit to be invaluable.

Back in Chapter One, I said how important it is that strategy be simple, and that is the real key to this. In addition to that, it has to be quick and inexpensive to do. Looked at it another way, if it took forever and cost a fortune in consultants' fees, would it ever get done? If you are a small to medium sized business, probably not.

From my experience in advising many businesses around the world, I find there are two completely opposite schools of thought when it comes to strategic planning. The first of which is to create a large quantity of paperwork, usually done by a team of expensive external consultants, which is supported with complex business plans containing hundreds of pages. Wow, it must be good, there is so much of it!

Inevitably this expensive and worthy document is far too valuable to risk being damaged, or exposed to the light, so it is kept well away from the mere mortals in charge of the day-to-day running of the business.

The logic is that, as long as you have created this important document and it is safely locked away, strategy has been put to bed, and you can concentrate on more important things, like running the business! Hmmmm.

Put this way, it does appear more than a little short- sighted, however, so often when I speak in front of chief executive forums and I ask, "Hands up who has ever written a business plan," of which quite a number raise their hands, then I follow up with, "How many have a current business plan?" of which hands start to drop and then finally, "How many are using it day-to- day to execute strategy on your business?".

Very few hands, if any are left, then I deliver the killer blow, "And where is it right now?" Usually a few responses of in a drawer, filing cabinet, on laptop, filed somewhere, and quite a few nods around the room and a couple of chuckles. The plan is usually sitting in the cloud, a drawer or a filing cabinet gathering dust and not being used. Because the moment a business plan is written, it's out of date.

So what is needed is a tool that is far more dynamic basis and a tool that can change and adapt over time. A tool like, well, **Strategy on a Page**™

The second and other extreme view of strategic planning is a polar opposite, the "back of a fag packet" or sometimes a beer mat.

I have found that, in working with entrepreneurs typically when they have ideas or concepts, they reach for whatever happens to be close in order to capture the thought. By contrast to the first example where verbosity rules, this is the complete opposite. Once the nearest scrap of material is found, a few illegible squiggles is all that is necessary to capture the company strategy for the year ahead. This is actually worse than not having any plan at all, because you have created the illusion that you have done the job, and can move onto more pressing things.

I have a rule these days if people come to me with a brand new start-up idea to help raise capital: I want to see a plan, written down. If you don't have one, I won't work with you – simple. Why so harsh? Simply put, if you can't be arsed to write down and gather your thoughts properly and coherently and have some semblance of a plan, why should I be bothered to help you find money? It's lazy. So many people have come to me with "ideas" wanting to raise capital, and I send them away with their tails between their legs and tell them to come back when they have a plan, and it doesn't need to be even a good one, just the start of one. I very rarely see those people again and they very rarely actually ever do anything with that idea. Ideas are plentiful, strategy is much rarer and flawless execution is becoming extinct.

If you have some grand strategic plan or some grand illusion which you can't do anything about today or this month, I suggest it's just a dream, it's not actually a strategy.

Right now, the world we are living in is moving at a fast pace, and change is all around us. The marketplace is very dynamic and, as a result, strategy needs to be able to adapt and change with it. Being an SME at this time gives you a huge competitive advantage because you can adapt and be far more nimble than the larger organisation which is more set in its ways.
These days, if you write a business plan, because of the pace of change, it is probably out of date before the ink has dried. By contrast, **Strategy on a Page** allows strategy to emerge over time; it enables you to be flexible; and allows strategy to subtly change as market dynamics change.

So where does **Strategy on a Page** come from? For me, it started many years ago when I was working for the global confectionery giant, Mars Incorporated. My first introduction to Strategy on a Page was on a large A3 sheet with very tiny text.

A super tanker takes almost three miles to come to a halt, even with the engines on full reverse.

A small vessel, just like an SME, is much closer to the water and can change course and adapt to the winds and tides in seconds.

You could get thousands of words on the page, but you almost needed a magnifying glass to read them. Not the easiest tool to use, but the principle has potential.

Later on, after I had left Mars and started my journey through the corporate world, I came across other versions of the same idea. Often they were far too complex and done to impress, rather than be used as a practical tool.

The result was that again it ended up not being used.

Even with the huge resources that the corporations I came across had thrown behind their strategies and plans, their investment was largely being wasted. The more you complicate things, the more likelihood is that they won't get used and things won't get done. No SME can afford that luxury.

Key Points

- Having a strategic plan helps entrepreneurs to stay on track and stops you from chasing all opportunities

- Strategy needs to be able to adapt to the fast-paced dynamics in business

- Strategic planning is essential to large corporations and SMEs

IF YOU WANT TO TEACH A MAN SOMETHING, DON'T TRY TO TEACH HIM. INSTEAD GIVE HIM A TOOL WHICH WILL GIVE HIM NEW WAYS OF THINKING. SCIENTIST AND INVENTOR BUCKMINSTER FULLER

"We are at our very best, and we are happiest, when we are fully engaged in work we enjoy on the journey toward the goal we've established for ourselves. It gives meaning to our time off and comfort to our sleep. It makes everything else in life so wonderful, so worthwhile."

Earl Nightingale

Chapter Three

Purpose

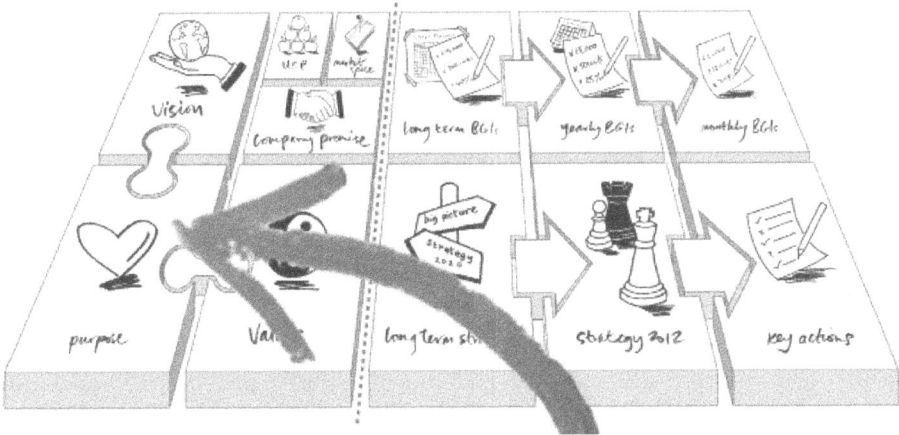

In 1902, author Rudyard Kipling wrote a series of cautionary tales call the "Just So Stories." One of these was titled, "The Elephant's Child" and it was there that this timeless piece of wisdom was written.

"I keep six honest serving-men (They taught me all I knew): Their names are What and Why and When And How and Where and Who."

But of all these six, to me the most important is "Why".

Why is the reason we do anything? Without a clear purpose, nothing happens. That is why this chapter is next, and why I believe it is so important.

If you get this bit right, everything flows.

Get this wrong, and you might just build the wrong business and find yourself trapped for the rest of your life and not be able to get out of it. There are all too many examples where this was the case.

Have you read Michael E Gerber's excellent book "The E-Myth"? In it he describes a scenario where somebody is in a technical job, like for instance, a hairdresser who gets fed up working for a boss and thinks they will be better off by

setting up their own hairdressing business. So they leave, and take the plunge into setting up their own business.

Many years later, they often find themselves trapped in that business because the part of it they actually liked was the technical bit, the hairdressing and the relationships with their customers. The bit that they didn't like was the running-the-business bit, so they have nowhere to go. Having a clear understanding of their true purpose would have saved them from this fate.

So why is purpose so important and why do I start with it? I even made it the strapline of my business, "Business Strategy with Purpose".

Anyone who I have consulted with over the years will know that I specialise in asking really searching and sometimes uncomfortable questions. I do so, not because I want to put anyone through a third degree unnecessarily, but because I know that it is the only way for them to gain complete clarity. So let me ask you some fundamental questions. I will know how serious you are if you read them, and then start to read on without answering them! The answer to these questions is completely fundamental and if you can't answer them to your complete satisfaction, then I would stop reading the book, and work on this until you can answer them. I have even provided some space here for you to write them in – and you have my permission to do so!

You can succeed in any business by just working half days. It doesn't matter which 12 hours you choose

---

Five Vital Questions you need to know the answers to.

Why do you exist as a company?

Why was the company set up?

- What's it meant to do for you?

- What does the end result look like?

- And what does exit look like?

Write your answers down before reading on.

These are fundamental questions which very few business owners ever ask, particularly the one about exit.

Whatever you start, you should do so with the end in mind.

Now, this book is predominantly about what we do whilst we're here living, but it is important to spend a few moments looking ahead and an exit strategy.

Let me ask you the question? Have you got an exit plan for your business? Or do you intend to exit your business? It is a serious question that may not be comfortable to contemplate.

When I'm talking to managing directors and chief execs and ask this question, very rarely do I get more than a couple of people putting up their hands.

Then I make the very bold statement that every single person in this room will exit their business whether they like it or not, and it's true. We will all exit our business. The only question is whether we do so in a coffin or in a taxi to the airport. The time to plan for that is now, whilst you have the time to influence the future that you want, and the legacy you want to leave.

In my experience, I would say that the majority of business owners started their business in order to provide a certain amount of finance and safety and security and abundance for their family, both now and in future. Ironically, though, if we do not put the right systems in place, the very vehicle that you are setting up to create the freedom that you want for your family could be the very vehicle that leaves your family impoverished when you go and traps you along the way.

If you do not have the right succession plans or the right exit plans in place on your business, and you do happen to die, then you leave a very very big problem for the family left behind. The problem may be so complex that it probably won't be unravelled. As a result, the business would collapse and may even leave your family with debts and problems in your wake. That's just from poor planning, and poor strategy. That is why this stuff is so important.

So, when we're looking at the long term strategy, it is really important to have your preferred exit scenario clearly in mind and to picture what that looks like, and you have a number of choices.

For example, one solution is indeed to sell. You build a company over three to five years with a clear plan to exit, sell

on to somebody else and then probably set up another one. That's very much the mark of a serial entrepreneur.

For many SMEs, the mindset would be different. For them, it is a lifestyle business and built around their passions and what they really enjoy. They are in this for life and so need to have a different strategy in place, such as the exit of self or removal of self over time.

This means just putting in and layering in the right senior management team within the company so that, maybe within three to five years, you can exit yourself and leave the company in good hands.

You would still own the company and maybe act as chair person or chairman or even as a non-executive director, but the company effectively runs itself and you just reap the dividends.

DERI AP JOHN LLEWELLYN DAVIES

The important thing is that you have the choice of having some active involvement if you wish, but it's entirely up to you. Giving yourself choices is the key thing in exit.

I once worked with clients who had belatedly started to look at the options open to them for an exit. Their objective was to look at making their exit plans within two to three years. At this point they were already in their sixties and they felt that it was time to come out. The problem was the business they'd created was the wrong business. They were heavily reliant on one client and the client was between 80% and 90% of their business, depending on the month, and as a result it was a very non-exitable business.

On top of that, the senior leaders had also boxed themselves into the organisation; they ran it, it was all about them. They

hadn't put any succession plans in place. So if you actually removed them from the business, the business would collapse. Now this wasn't a problem, and a solution could be found, but not in such a short period of time.

So with these guys, they wanted to exit with a clean set of heels in 18 months, but the reality was they didn't have the right succession plans and they didn't have the right client structure to be able to do so. Now we could do that in three to five years ,which is what we are working on, but if that

had been planned several years in advance, we would have the desired outcome already and they would be retired, sipping margaritas in Barbados.

Exit is too important to leave to the last minute. (ps – this client successfully exited in 2.5 years)

These five core elements will ensure that you are building the right business with the right strategy.

- Passion
- Service and Value
- Opportunity
- Financial
- Lifestyle

So now, let's take each one of those in turn

1.   Passion

What are you good at?	*What do people think you are good at?*

The Zone of Mediocrity and Regret

The Circle of Passion

The Zone of Hope and Unexplored Passion

What do you really love to do?	*What do you feel you should be doing?*

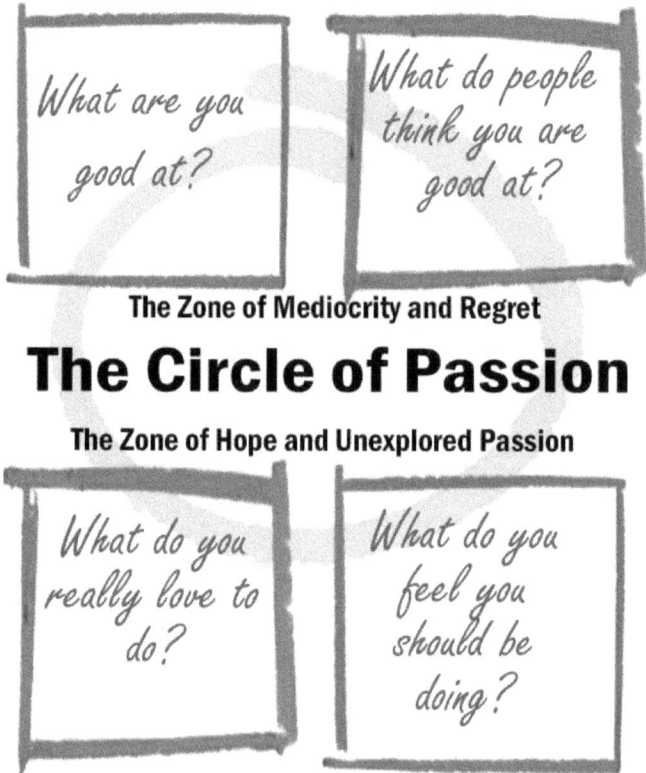

When I am choosing clients to work with, the first thing that I look for is Passion. Do they love what they do?

If we don't love what we do, why are we doing it? Life is so short, and this world is so abundant with

Opportunities that not actually spending your time doing something that you really enjoy doing and having fun at the same time just seems futile

The flip side of that is that, when the bad times come, and they inevitably will come because all of us face troubles along the way, if you are not passionate and enjoy what you do,

then you will give up. It is that burning passion behind what you do and the bigger purpose behind it all that keeps entrepreneurs' spirits up even through the darkest of times.

- **The Zone of Mediocrity and Regret**
- **The Circle of Passion**
- **The Zone of Hope and Unexplored Passion**

What are you good at?

What do people think you are good at?

What do you really love to do?

What do you feel you should be

What do you feel you should be doing?

So where do you get your passion from? I do an exercise in speaking forums called the Circle of Passion.

This is how it works.

The first quadrant is titled, "What are you good at?" and the one beside it is, "What do people think you're good at?" They may not be the same! Anyway, let's look at the second two points of passion. More questions, I'm afraid, so brace yourself! The next two questions are,

What do you really love to do?

What do you feel you should be doing?

Now, I don't mean to use the word 'should' in the sense of it being an obligation, more of a deep feeling inside, in the very essence of who you are.

Instinctively, what do you feel like you should be doing that you're not doing now?

What's your calling?

What is your soul telling you that you should be doing right now?

Spend a moment thinking about it and put your first thoughts down on paper – before your mind has a chance to edit or modify them.

Now, this I see as the zone of hope and the unexplored. A lot of times we love things but we don't follow them through. A lot of times we feel we should be doing something with our lives, maybe we should be taking a different career choice, but for whatever reason we choose not to do it.

Of course, it doesn't logically follow that just because you love something and you feel that you should be doing it, it doesn't actually necessarily mean you're good at it.

I did this exercise on myself, a long time ago. I knew I loved adventure, I knew I loved being out in the outdoors and exploring, and I also felt that I should be doing it, but I wasn't.

When I came to my high mountaineering exploits, I discovered that I wasn't good at it at all. In fact, I was quite rubbish at it. If you read my book, "Life's Great Adventure," you'll see the journey that I went on and you'll realise that I am not making this up! Even my mountain guides thought I was rubbish too. Thanks, guys!

So just because you love to do something and you feel you should be doing it, it does not necessarily mean you're going to be good at it yet.

However, with enough discipline, with enough drive and enough application, you can be good at anything you choose, and that's when all the links start to come together.

If you look at me, you'll know that I actually love strategy. I'm a strategy geek! You'll see this when I speak and it is the reason why I'm writing this book. I have a real passion for strategy and I feel like I should be doing it and it has enabled me to fulfil a calling of mine, to help, advise, and empower SMEs.

Going back to the diagram, strategy is something I'm good at because of all my experience in this field, and other people now think I'm good at it. That's how the circle of passion really connects when all four quadrants start to flow into one.

The really important lesson you need to take out of this is that you should really love what you do. If you're in a business

and you realise this is lacking, that's fine for now, but you really need to work on an exit strategy to get you out, so you can find your true purpose and do something you do really love to do.

Also, be careful and don't confuse hobbies with business (more on this in a moment). They are different but sometimes in true mastery of this, they blend into one, like adventure has for me.

"Strong lives are motivated by dynamic purposes; lesser ones exist onwishes and inclinations."

Kenneth Hildebrand

2. Service and Value

I really believe in the fact that no matter what we do, whatever we're offering in life, we should all be adding real service and real value. True wealth comes from a multiplier of service and value, times leverage.

If we're really, really adding value, then depending on how many people we can touch with that value determines our wealth. Let's have a think of a few people here.

If you think about Bill Gates, does he add service and does he add value with what they've created within Microsoft? Well, every time you touch a computer right now, you're probably touching some form of Microsoft application. They've helped business, they've helped automate business and they've added huge service around the planet. Bill Gates is wealthy as a direct result.

So just think about what is your service? How are you adding value to your customers? If you are struggling to answer that, or cannot do so with real passion and say why your service or products are so valuable, then you've got a fundamental hole in the business.

I also touch here on philanthropy because if you're a charity or a social enterprise, the service you're adding will be of a philanthropic nature and it will be subtly different. But nevertheless, it is still a service, a huge one. So think about what is the actual service and the value that you're adding within your business.

3. Opportunity

What is the opportunity in the market space for your passion and your service? Here's the thing. You can absolutely love to do something and you could be giving a service in doing it. But if there's no market opportunity out there for you to capitalise on, then you have a hobby. Don't get me wrong, a hobby's fine and a lot of businesses I've come across are hobby businesses, but just understand that is what it is.

So, check out the market space, understand both the opportunity and also the size of the opportunity, and make sure that your service and value are aligned according to it.

If you have those three things running, if you have a passion for what you do, you're adding huge service and value in doing it and there's an opportunity in the market space for you to capitalise on, then this triggers the penultimate piece of the purpose which is, Financial purpose.

> "If you make a sale,
> you make a living.
> If you make an investment of
> time and good service in a
> customer,
> you can make a fortune."
> *Jim Rohn*

4. Financial purpose

Part of the purpose should always be financial. I don't care what this financial metric is, whether a modest income or a multimillion pound sell-out, and I work with both. The most important part is that it's the right financial reward for you and profit is central to this.

A lot of people get stuck on this, and it is a book in its own right, but for simplicity think of it this way: how much money do you need to deliver the lifestyle of your choosing?

The house, the car, the holiday, the kids etc. Put a figure on it in asset terms and income terms, as this will drive the business growth indicators later.

If your business can't deliver the financial rewards that you set out for, you have two choices: choose another business or refine your lifestyle in the knowledge that you will be doing something you love.
Here's the sad thing: a lot of people get locked into a lifestyle of materialism, competing with the Jones's and getting bigger toys.

They spend their lives accumulating and can't wait for retirement as they hate what they do. They then retire and die in several years after truly wasting their passions and talent.

My dad died just a couple of years after retiring and this to me was a wake-up call. I made a pact that it would never happen to me and I would live this life fully every day.

5. Lifestyle

We should always understand what the business can generate and what the numbers are because, without it, you will not live the final purpose piece, the purpose, which is, Lifestyle.

If you take Mother Teresa, as an example. Did Mother Teresa have a Passion for what she did? I would say yes. Was she adding huge Service and philanthropy? Yes. Did she have an Opportunity to make a change and a difference in Calcutta, and around the world? Absolutely. And did she earn the right to a Financial Reward to live the Lifestyle that she chose? Again, yes.

Mother Teresa actually chose to live a very impoverished lifestyle, one that she was more than happy with. You never saw her complaining. She didn't need the money, she didn't expect the wealth, it wasn't part of what she needed. She lived the perfect lifestyle she chose to lead along with her passion and service in the place she has.

Again, now look at someone like Steve Jobs from Apple. Absolutely Passionate about what he did. He provided huge service through all the Apple products and offerings throughout the world and a massive Opportu- nity in the market space.

As a result, he gleaned huge Financial Reward and lived the Lifestyle that he chose along the way. However he alledgedly died with regret. So this is important work.

This is not about size or scale. Just ensure that all five elements of your purpose are covered.

I want you to think about these elements now and use some of the following case studies and examples to promote your thinking.

With the right purpose in place, and with clarity as to your future exit plans, then you are ready to start mapping strategy properly knowing that it's aligned to the right thing.

"Money is like manure; just piling it up does no good, you need to spread it around."

Key Points

- Purpose is the reason for which something is done or created or for which something exists'

- What are your elements of purpose?

- Why do you exist as a company?

- Have an exit plan even if you never use it

"Life without a mission
has no purpose
.Life without a purpose
is fruitless.
Find your mission,
live your purpose
and add value to life."

Chapter Four

Vision

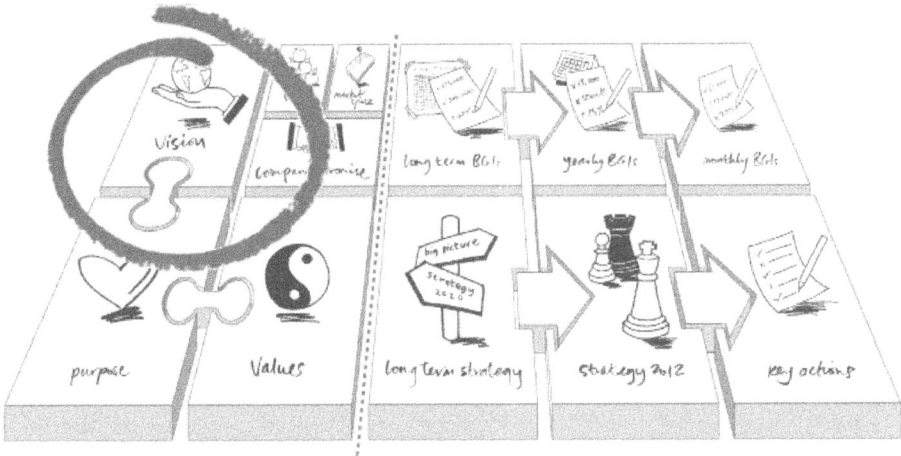

In the award-winning play and film by Arthur Miller, "Death of a Salesman" , there was the memorable line, "You've got to have a dream, boy. It comes with the territory."

If you are the leader of your organisation, large or small, it is your dream, your vision, that will drive it and inspire others to follow you.

Make no mistake about this, every big and worthwhile achievement started as a clear vision in the mind of one person. That vision, coupled with purpose and all the other elements that combine to create a strategy, is what has built the world around us. But the key here is that it all starts as a thought, the spark of an idea. A vision.

Many people underestimate the importance of mindset in business. For many, the world of Personal Development and the power of attitude appears a bit woolly and irrelevant to the big task of just getting on with the job. However, never underestimate the power of thought.

Thoughts are the building blocks of vision. Thoughts can also be positive or negative and both are equally powerful in the ways they can influence what we then choose to do.

"First comes thought; then organization of that thought; then transformation of those plans into reality. The beginning, as you will observe, is in your imagination."

In 2006, the Australian author Rhonda Byrne created a film and subsequently a book called "The Secret". The film was released online with a viral "word of mouth" campaign and shot round the world. The book has sold over 21 million copies and has been translated into 44 languages. The subject? The Law of Attraction and the power of positive thought.

"The Secret" describes the Law of Attraction as a natural law which determines the order of the universe through the process of "like attracts like".

For example, if you think angry thoughts and feel angry, you will attract back events and circumstances that cause you to feel more anger.

Conversely, if you think and feel positively, you will attract back positive events and circumstances.

Whatever you might feel about the concept of "natural laws", there is no doubt that the attitude that we choose to bring to any situation has a major influence on the attitude that others will have to us as a result.

I was once at an airport during a time when all flights were being cancelled or delayed. It was chaos! Looking around me, I saw the hard-pressed airline staff, being roundly abused and shouted at for circumstances that were clearly not their fault. When I arrived at the desk, instead of adding to their woes, I was charming and sympathetic to them. The result was that they found me a flight on a different airline and got me on my way far quicker than could well have been the case. Choosing a positive approach does have practical advantages and does influence what happens next!

As Rhonda Byrne writes, "One of the most powerful uses of gratitude can be incorporated in the Creative Process to turbo-charge what you want."
The Law of Attraction is just one of what are known as The Natural Laws which appear to govern how we operate and the results that we achieve, but they are way beyond the context of this book. However, never forget, as Dr Wayne W. Dyer says, "You are the result of all the precious pictures you have painted for yourself....and you can always paint new ones!" Your vision is the key to your future.
Although it was Ralph Waldo Emerson who said, "We become what we think about all day," centuries before that, in 563 BC, it was Buddha who said, "We are shaped by our thoughts; we become what we think. When the mind is pure, joy follows like a shadow that never leaves." I can't argue with that

The Law of the Harvest

Sow a thought,
reap an act.
Sow an act,
reap a habit.
Sow a habit,
reap a character.
Sow a character,
reap a destiny.

What does your future look like?

What do people use to help them focus on their vision of the future? Many create a "Dream Board" in their kitchen or on the wall in their office. On it, they tend to put pictures cut out from magazines of the things they really want – or think that they really want!

It appears to be a man thing to put up pictures of fast cars, speed boats, palatial houses or exotic holidays. Very rarely do you see a Dream Board with the vision for the business portrayed with such strong visuals. If only it were, how powerful would that be in reminding us every day of the future we dream about?

But wait a minute – that is exactly what you have with Strategy on a Page It is not only your Dream Board for you and your business, but a road map to take you there. So the question is, where do you want it to take you in three, five or ten years? What does that picture look like?

Inventing your future

If you are to achieve your vision of the future, it needs to be specific. The more specific it is, the easier it will be to achieve. If it is specific, it can be written down and a time frame applied to it.

So what does short term, medium term and long term mean to you? In some fast moving industries like IT, a year can be a lifetime. You know this to be true because whenever you buy the latest gadget in the shops, by the time you get it home, it is already out of date and the next version is being created.

In some countries, like Japan, that take a commendably long term view, their definition of long term might well be 100 years. Depending on your industry, your long term may by five years or ten years. But whatever it means, define it. Write it down.

So, what is the vision for your business in the long term? What does it look like?

What can you see? Who is with you? Where are you? What are the different elements that now make up your business?

Take a moment, close your eyes and picture it clearly in your mind. Then write it down.

Now I know that everybody is different so to help you gain clarity, and to express your own vision, here are some common elements that might give you a guide.

Your Brand

If you were to define what Brand means, you might say, "A design, a logo or a particular feature that uniquely identifies that business or product." In my view though, it is much more than that.

It is also about the image associated with it, the culture and the values it represents in the marketplace. In a small business, you may well be your own brand. You and your company may be inextricably linked in the mind of your customers. In the context of Vision, you need to know what it means to you and what you want it to represent to others. If not yet now, in the future.

So much about brand is unseen and is a reflection of the way that people feel when interacting with you or your team. Ask yourself, after a long and frustrating telephone call with a call centre halfway around the world acting on behalf of a major company, how were you left feeling about their brand? Every small point of contact with a customer is an opportunity to add to their feelings towards your brand, or of subtracting from it.

The legendary marketeer and world class copywriter, Drayton Bird, tells a story of a person attending a huge international congress. He walked into a room of one thousand people and didn't know anybody, except one person who he spotted, but couldn't stand. So who did he talk to? The one person he knew but couldn't stand.

Now, think of that in the context of a brand. In a crowded marketplace with a proliferation of suppliers, we also will gravitate to the ones we know and feel comfortable with. The secret is for them to come to your brand because of it – not despite it!

Brand Values

So how do you want your brand to be perceived?

- What are your brand values?
- Where would you like people to position you in the marketplace?
- What aspect of your brand will make the biggest difference when people choose to do business with you?
- If your brand were an animal, what would it be? (Don't say a shark!)

Your standing in the Marketplace

Gaining prominence for your business is achieved in many ways. If you are perceived to be at the cutting edge of your particular world, then that is one way of creating a differentiator. If your brand has gained national recognition by winning an industry award or is seen as being outstanding in their field, it also makes a big difference. However, as they used to say about the National Lottery, "You've got to be in it to win it."

In order to put yourself in contention for that sort of recognition, you need to be a part of those organisations, professional or trade bodies who run the awards. You need to put yourself in harm's way to get noticed – and for all the right reasons.

A number of my clients are now winning awards when they hadn't beforehand. The reason? They now have a vision to do so, and are doing something about it, nothing more….

How your customers feel about you is really important. Do you know? Have you asked them?

Do you have the sort of feedback mechanism in place that your customers feel comfortable to use?

Do you use that feedback to fine-tune your offering and your service?

If a part of your vision is all about how your organisation will be perceived in the future, you need to be able to measure that now, and at regular intervals, so that you can move closer to achieving that vision in the future.

The greater clarity you have on all of this, the easier it will be for you to articulate and share your vision and inspire others to believe in it.

The Dream Office

Just like the pictures on the fridge of the sports cars and the yacht, so many people's vision for their business is for it to occupy a prestigious space, with a big reception area, and acres of glass and chrome. What is your vision for where your business will be situated? What does it look like in your mind?

We all spend too much time in our work environment so it is important that it is fit for purpose and positively contributes to what it is we are trying to achieve. There is a growing trend for many growing businesses to work out of a home office and to have a virtual team of other specialists in support, all doing the same thing.

For me, I work out of my Pall Mall clubs. I find the ambience and the luxuriousness of them suits my personality. They are a home from home and I feel wonderful as I walk through the door. I know that when I invite a client to come and join me there for a meeting, they will feel the same way, which is important. Whilst when I am working from home, I do so from a bespoke office that looks over the rolling countryside. I also do most of my phone calls whilst backpacking through the wye valley or herefordshire. That's why I am panting a bit; I'm not heavy breathing, honest ;-)

When you are passionate about what you do and love to share that passion, you need to have a place to work in that you can be proud of. So what is your vision for that?

Some people like to have big trendy offices with large boards outside showing off their branding. Is that important to you? I was very lucky to have had Google as a client a number of years ago and visited them in their offices in Dublin which were situated, it appeared, in some kind of a play park. There were tents, games and all sort of unbusinesslike furniture all over their offices. It was an amazingly creative space. Imagine how their staff must feel working there?

I visited a top advertising agency in Sydney, Australia. After our meeting, we were taken to the top floor where they had a fantastic bar overlooking Sydney Harbour.
It was filled with floor cushions, sofas and loungers in a very creative space, not the sort of thing you would expect to find in a place of work. But what was the work? Being creative! So maybe they had it exactly right.

What is your vision of the perfect space for your business? Write it down!

Of course, your vision might be more geographical. You might see yourself in multiple cities around the world in the future and gaining recognition for what you do across many different continents.

Whatever you do, never think small. Your vision can be awesomely and outrageously large! And why not? If you aim for the stars, you might hit the moon!

Are you a Smooth Operator?

Operations are never a sexy subject, but having a clear vision for them is also vital.

- **What is going to make your company tick?**
- **What will it need to be scalable?**
- **What will it take to deliver a predictable, quality customer experience?**
- **What sort of people will you need to attract in order to deliver your vision?**

Get a clear picture of what this will look like in the future and write it down.

Many business leaders are called Visionaries.
This is because they had great clarity on a simple concept and were able to communicate it in such a way that inspired others to make it happen.

So, are you getting a clear Vision for your business yet? Even the most beautiful of statues started as a big lump of rock. All you need to do is to discard anything that doesn't look like your vision of the statue.

One thing that that might help you to do this is to visualise the point in the future when you might choose to exit from your business. It might be in just three years' time. If you were writing that prospectus now, how would you be describing the business to prospective purchasers?

- What size has it grown to?
- Who is a part of your business?
- What is the business delivering?
- What is it's position in the marketplace?
- What are competitors saying about you?
- What industry recognition have you attracted?
- What are customers saying about you?
- What do your offices look like, and where are they?
- What will realising the sale of this asset help you to achieve next?

Of course, the last thing on your mind might be an exit strategy, but sometimes this process can help the fog to clear a little.

Whatever you write down as your Vision, you are not carving it into a tablet of stone. As time progresses, you will learn from the dynamics of your business, from what your competitors are doing, gain greater clarity from what is happening in the marketplace and from the feedback of your customers and staff. So do not fall into the trap of doing this once, then forgetting about it. Make a note in your diary to revisit in three months' time and check that it is still accurate. Your Purpose, Vision and Values (which we will be looking at shortly) are the ECG of your business. Without them, there can be no pulse or respiration – and you know what that means! Your vision has to excite you and be an inspiring expression of what you are planning to become and achieve. It also has to be sensitive enough to notice change and trends, and flexible enough to accommodate them.

I know I am harping on at this, but as you can see it is my passion. If I can get you as excited as I am about this stuff, I know the difference it will make to your future. This is why it is so important, at the start of any enterprise, to have complete clarity. Everything worthwhile starts with Vision and Purpose, and it is not just for your benefit.

Vision and Purpose help to paint a picture to your employees, suppliers, partners, investors and customers about your quest. It gives them the opportunity to align themselves with you and to help by contributing towards reaching your stated goals.

People will follow you through the building-of-the-foundations stage because they have a clear picture of what the completed building will look like.

Vision in Action

Let me tell you the story of Molly Bedingfield, the founder of the charity Global Angels who I was blessed to serve on their international advisory board. For over 20 years she worked closely with charity projects all over the world as part of a movement of social entrepreneurs developing sustainable and holistic models of change. Their values united their passion to facilitate impoverished communities to break the cycle of poverty, village by village, country by country.

She was concerned that, despite the billions spent on aid in recent years, the number of people suffering around the world has grown to an astronomical level.

Convinced that the old models of charity didn't work, Molly was sure something needed to be done to change the course of history for ALL children. Her vision was to create a new kind of charity with a different business model that was transparent and connected with today's informed givers.

Thinking through the vision and strategy for such a charitable foundation, she created the concept of Global Angels as a significant people movement, facilitating positive change.

But her vision went further still. She was aware that the current business model of many charities was not transparent and it was almost impossible to know how much of any donation went on administration cost, salaries and expenses. Molly came up with the powerful offering of the 100% Promise.

The global Angels Charity was built on the promise that 100% of all money donated went directly to projects. None of it was to go to administrative costs or overheads.

All of those costs would be covered by Angel Partners, Corporate Angels and patrons.

A radical concept with a vision to attract donations of over 100 million pounds plus the support and endorsement of world leaders who contribute their time and connections to help projects achieve their objectives! WOW, what a vision and Molly is well on the way to realising it.

All of this was built on very clear Vision, Purpose and Values and has both inspired and helped thousands. It all started with just one small idea which was shared and which then blossomed and grew.

With the same clarity of vision, and a Strategy to drive it, is there anything that you too, could not accomplish? Everyone Can Be An Angel

It was essential that everyone could be involved and enjoy their partnership with the charity and hence adopted the slogan, "Everyone can be an Angel".

To build the foundations of a charity that would be able to expand rapidly, we needed to be adaptable and innovative in changing times and lean on operating costs.

Our vetting procedure and monitoring of charity projects partners needed to be excellent, yet simple. We adopted a strategy of collaborating with, and outsourcing to, experts and skilled volunteers, who would form our wider Global Angels Team. This would bring in high-level key skills, keep costs down and provide the opportunity for many people to donate their services as Angels. Companies and individuals would be invited to sponsor our operating costs or donate resources as Corporate Angels.

Key Points

- Vision is the expression of your purpose, what it looks like

- Your thoughts are the building blocks of vision, so keep them focused and positive

- Visualise and experience how you want your company to be by visiting others in your industry for inspiration

- Your brand is the visual representation of your vision, so make sure that it is aligned

- What systems and operations need to be in place for your vision to be fulfilled?

Chapter Five

Values

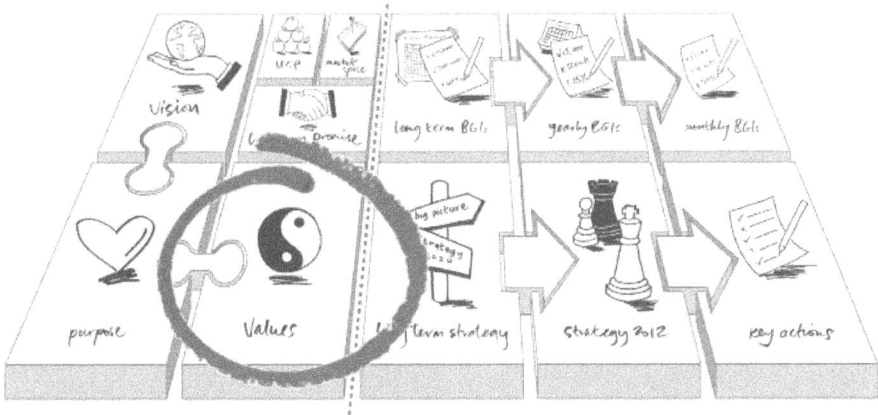

"I f we are to go forward, we must go back and rediscover those precious values - that all reality hinges on moral foundations and that all reality has spiritual control."
Martin Luther King, Jr.

Now, before the hardened business veterans out there start rolling their eyelids and thinking we're about to enter into a very fluffy chapter based on fluffy values and niceness, I want to begin this chapter with a very, very serious point. This is probably one of the most important parts of the page and if you get this bit right, the amount of energy, expenditure and general enjoyment of business life will increase tremendously.

So when I'm talking about values, I'm not talking about some fluffy set of words that stick on a wall and don't mean anything. For me, this is a very, very serious section, so serious that crossing values and lack of values is a sackable offence.

So, what do we mean by values? I talk about values in different ways in different places. So let me put in context what I mean by values in terms of Business Growth International and Strategy on a Page

There is quite a powerful movement in the personal development or personal growth industry based around values and, in this way, it's defined in terms of what we value in life and where we spend our time. I think there are many true masters in the world at expressing values in this way including a dear friend of mine Jo simpson (go to the only resources **www.strategyonapage.biz** for more on jo and values)

Her philosophies are key in the grander scheme of life but they are not the values we're talking about For your page.

Her philosophies are key in the grander scheme of life but they are not the values we're talking about For your page

The values we're talking about here are the values specifically for business, otherwise it would be termed something else, such as traits, or expectations. But coming out of the corporate world, it's typically been called values. I like this terminology because, for me, it resonates. But if it doesn't resonate for you and you want to call it something else, that's fine. Somebody I worked with recently wanted to call it Ethos and I'm fine with that too. Again, I don't care if you call it an Aardvark as long as it works for you.

So, what do we mean here? It is about expectation, and how we expect ourselves to behave and how we expect our staff, our partners, our customers to behave around us. It's our expectations of behaviour. It's what we do, it's our daily doing, this is the way we actually portray ourselves and also what we won't tolerate around us, what we expect and what we won't put up with.

The words we use are very important, but never forget that they can mean different things to different people, so you have to make the meaning clear.

For example, to describe what you mean by integrity, you might say, "We always tell the truth, we never try to hide things and we take full responsibility for our actions." That statement means a lot more than just a single word *integrity* and it's very explicit in what we mean by it.

With all the many companies that I have worked with over the years, all of them have a different set of words to describe their values. No two have been the same.

So how do we get to values? How do we actually elicit what values are? It is very easy to spend a lot of time on this and there are plenty of great coaches and leadership gurus out there who can help you to go a lot deeper into this area. However, that's not the point of the page. Right now, we need to understand and put into words what the values of your business really are, in as quick a way as possible.

Describing the Values
of the Business

When I am working within a company, one of the ways that I help them to understand their values is to ask about the last time they had to fire somebody.

If you're a leader in your organisation then at some point I'm sure you've had to get rid of someone. I've certainly had to get rid of many people in my time. Not a job that I enjoy, but a necessary one as part of leadership.

When it happens it means that we have exhausted all the other processes leading up to taking that decision, not that it will have happened lightly. It is a sure sign then that they've crossed the line regarding the values of the organisation. If you can pinpoint the values they've crossed, then all you need to do is to flip the side of that to discover the positive values they represent.

For instance, a company I was working with recently had to fire a guy because he was lazy. He didn't do the job he said he was going to do, was always late on his delivery, and was always late coming into the office.

So when we flipped those things around, we discovered that the positive values we were looking for were that we wanted someone who's energised, and who's loving what they do. In addition, we also wanted the values of delivering on time, all the time, and having pride in their work and the respect for company time.

So, if we can elicit why we got rid of somebody in the past, make sure we don't make the same mistake again in the future by having a clear set of values to use when recruiting.

The second question I ask is, "Who's the last person who really annoyed you in business, and why?" Even if you are quite an amiable person, this may be a rarity, but if you can remember the last person to have peeved or miffed you, it's a sure sign that they've crossed your values. Again, if you flip that to find the positive, you get an understanding of a value that is important to you.

One value that most companies regard as fundamental is Time. Surprisingly though, few of them actually spell this out and just expect people to realise it for themselves. Managers get annoyed when people turn up late or appear to be unreliable timekeepers. They sit behind their desks moaning about behaviours of certain staff members without actually explicitly telling them what their expectations of that behaviour is.

Poor timekeeping was a major problem for a company that I worked with once. People turned up late all the time and there was a high proportion of sick leave. When I challenged them with this and asked them how there were addressing the problem, they admitted that they were not doing anything about it. Moreover, they had never really spelt out to staff that this was not acceptable behaviour.

The current system was that if somebody was late or going to be late in the morning, the only thing they had to do was text their mate, or text the person opposite them saying that, well, "I'm going to be fifteen minutes late this morning." The same process applied when somebody was going to be off sick. If you were sick, all you needed to do was to text somebody in the office, usually the most junior person, to say, "I'm going to be off sick today."

What we did was put a very clear campaign in place which started with communicating the importance of time to the company as a whole. We expressed it as part of the values of the business and how, if you were fifteen minutes late, it was the company time that you were stealing. Not only that but you were letting the whole team down, and somebody would have to take your workload while you were not there.

We explained clearly why time was important and that poor timekeeping both let down your team and cost the company money. It was not acceptable.

So next, we then put in a new regime where, if you were going to be late, you had to text the CEO, not one of your mates. Not surprisingly, this had a dramatic effect!

When do we use Values?

Now, there were just fifteen people in this company, so texting the CEO wasn't a big deal. I don't recommend this if you have 2,000 people in your company, but having to text or telephone the main boss if you're going to be late, or absent because of sickness, does focus the mind and means you've got to have a really good reason to do so.

By putting this simple communication process in place, reinforcing it regularly, and making it a lot more detrimental for you if you were going to be late, we pretty much eradicated lateness and sickness within two weeks. A major achievement and a noticeable difference to the bottom line.

The learning point from this was that, if there is something happening in the organisation that goes against your values, there's no point bitching and moaning about it, unless you're going to communicate it and express clearly and succinctly the behaviour you do expect

So when do we use values? In a small company, the values of the business are almost certainly those of the business owner and are championed by them to all of their staff.

With larger companies, the values will be typically still from the value of the original leader, but then will be expressed a little bit more around the values of the whole board. So getting values explicit and getting them through the current company is the first priority and the obvious way of expressing values.

One of the most effective places to use values is in the recruitment process when you bring new people into the company. During this process, most people recruit on the basis of a CV, where they are basing their decision on skills and what people can do.

In small companies, this is often a quick interview process, with one or sometimes two interviews to establish that they can do the job, and that's it.

Now, I take a different perspective. I'm taking it as read that they can do the job, and obviously we drill down to establish that very carefully. However, I am more interested in how well they will fit into the company and the values it represents. Values are why people get fired, so this is by far the best time to measure them in this regard.

Providing people have the right skill sets, most things can be trained. It's whether or not they have the 'want' or desire, and the right attitude to succeed.

Sometimes people have the skill to do the job, but they just don't do it because they don't have the drive, they don't have the right values in place, they don't have the work ethic. So we always, always recruit on values.

When you do this, and build a team that instinctively lives the values of the business, it very quickly shows up those people who are not. If left to their own devices, these 'internal terrorists' will slowly undermine your efforts and try to win people round to their negative outlook.

Internal terrorists

In any company of over about six or seven people, there's usually at least one terrorist quietly working away against you. The bigger the company becomes over time, the more senior the terrorist is likely to become if not identified and acted on. This is where you, as a leader, really need to have the strength to be able to either get rid of them or to work on changing their values over time.

Experience has shown me that it is very, very difficult to elicit a change in values over time so, if you do not get rid of these people, they can be responsible for creating a real bottleneck within your company.

As a leader, you probably already know the one person that you've got a problem with. You also probably know that you should have got rid of them by now, and you haven't.

Once you elicit values and you're clear on what they are, it will probably become very clear as to why you should be getting rid of that person. Not doing so will be far more costly to the business than letting them go. Trust me!

So, alignment to the true values of the company starts even before the recruitment process. It starts with the way you use your values to position your business in the marketplace and thus attract those people who are already aligned to your way of thinking.

Once you're clear on what your values are on the page, then you can elicit interview questions to test those values over time. In addition to this, I really advocate using psychometric profiling in the interview process. There are many excellent ones to choose from, so choose one that gives you an insight into the values held by the candidate.

The cost of getting it wrong during the recruitment process is vastly more than the cost of getting it right. Never grudge the investment in a psychometric profile.
It will always pay off.

If you're about to make thousands of pounds worth of recruitment decisions, spending a couple of hundred pounds to test values and test your skill set is really the best investment you can make in the recruitment process.

Recruiting customers who share your values

But values go beyond your current internal staff and the recruitment process. They go beyond that into the partners you choose. If you're going to go into a joint venture, if you're setting up a new business and you're thinking about bringing in business partners or new board members, it must all be based on values. I've seen whole companies crumble just because the directors all wanted to go in different directions because they had different values.

You also recruit your customers based on values. This is the biggest trick of them all and this is where people really struggle. I was just speaking in an executive forum on this very point when somebody in the room challenged me on it. "Surely you can't be selective with your customers?" he asked. I asked him if there was anyone on his customer base that was a real pain to deal with. And indeed there was. Over time, it is inevitable that a real nuisance customer will come along. Instinctively though, many businesses would think twice about sacking a customer and are scared about losing the business.

I just asked him, "What are the values that they're crossing?" He explained that they didn't value his time, and were always expecting things for free. There was just no respect or value placed on what he was doing. So I asked him has he ever told them this, and obviously he hadn't.

So we set a little challenge for him to go back to that customer. First of all, we clarified that he could afford to lose that customer. They weren't very big, but they caused most of his problems. So he went back to that customer and expressed his values to them and said, "Look, this is what I really need to feel valued in what I do and make sure that I'm adding value to you. It is important that there's a mutual respect between the two of us for the professionalism that we have. If you don't see the value that I'm giving and there's not a mutual respect, then it's probably better that we part our ways."

Interestingly, in this case, the customer apologised, and said that they didn't realise what they were doing. They changed their ways and now the relationship is good.

There will be times when, despite having this conversation, the values of your customer are so at odds with your own as

to make it too difficult do business with them. In this case, you should be prepared to accept that you have done everything possible, and be prepared to go your separate ways.

The one criteria that I use when selecting my clients is their values. Purpose and vision are key as well, but values are number one, and that is what they all need to share.

They all need to share a common set of values that's all based around respect and value and action. If that is not the case, then we simply couldn't work together.

So as you can see again, values isn't just a once a year exercise to be written down and put in a drawer. It is something that plays a major part in the life of the company every single day, every single week, every single month.

Case Study on Values

I recently did an exercise on Values with Glenn Burgess and Jeff Spires, two very talented and enthusiastic partners in Pow New Media, which provides solutions in the world of SEO, digital marketing and pay-per-click.

The exercise produced a really exciting set of values, which included Integrity and Transparency. However, there was one value that I challenged them with which was 'delivering massive values and going that extra mile' . On the face of it, a very powerful value to have.

I let this ride for a few months whilst I watched the underlying business model at work and it became clear that they were lacking in profitability in some of the jobs they were doing.

They were doing the jobs, which seemed amazingly profitable at the beginning and the outset, but when you actually tracked it against reality, the profitability was being eroded over time. This was actually due to one of the values they had set themselves, which was delivering massive value and always going the extra mile.

Well, if you're always going the extra mile, then at some point that has to impact on profitability.

We discussed this and agreed to reword this value to read, "We always deliver massive value. We create raving fans whilst being profitable."

Now, this changed things around in the thinking of the way

they priced projects, the way they delivered projects and the way they put value on themselves and what they did. Because if you're always going the extra mile, you're always delivering more than is expected and therefore, you're probably losing profitability as a result.

That's a great example of having to be very careful with our values because, if you are not careful, some values can be detrimental.

This is why, a lot of the time, strategy's not executed because the correct values aren't in place to underpin it.

Key Points

- Values are expectations or traits that you look for in other people

- They are not an exercise you do once a year. Acting contrary to company values is a sackable offence

- The values of a company should be lived every day, from the CEO to the secretary

- You should also recruit people based on the company's values;; from staff to suppliers

- Joint venture partners, investors and customers will be attracted to you if you market your values and they align with yours

---

Chapter Six

Your unique business

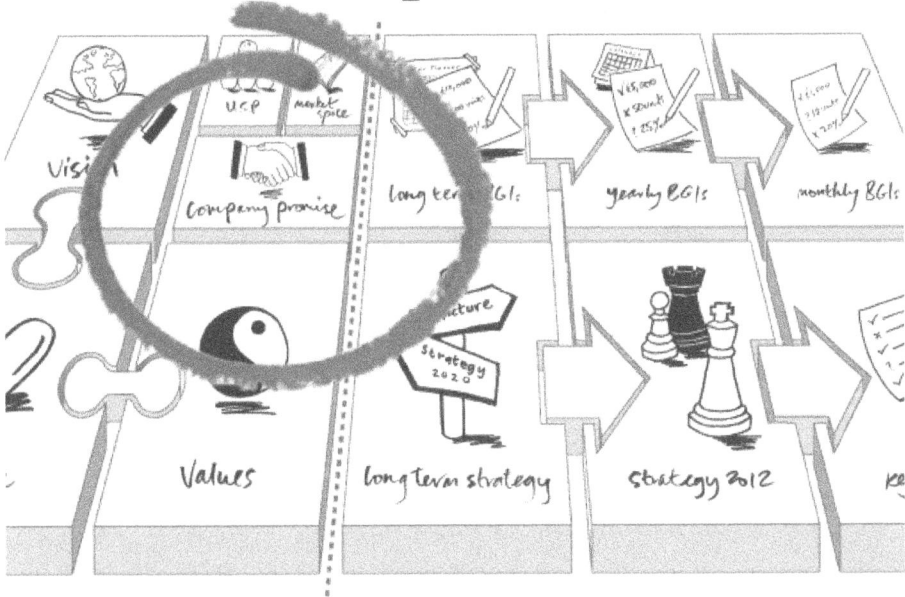

"Not everybody can be famous but everybody can be great, because greatness is determined by service."
Martin Luther King, Jr.

So far in the first four chapters, we have covered the first two elements of our BGI Strategy on a PageTM; the Vision and the Purpose. Now we move up to the second square on the top line of the diagram, which is split into three areas;

Unique Selling Proposition
Market Space
Company promise

Although they have not been allocated a large amount of space on the diagram, they are nevertheless powerful individual elements of the bigger picture and each serve an important purpose.

It's a big world out there!

The subconscious brain has a lot to answer for. It very effectively filters the torrent of data that flows over us every day and bring to our attention only those items that we have told it we are interested in knowing about.

It is a bit like the new generation of video recorders that record the programmes you don't like and plays them back when you are out.

Seriously, if it wasn't for our internal filter we would drown under information. The downside is that it can work against us as well. For example, if you hear an unusual name that you've not heard before, all of a sudden you become aware of that name popping up all over the place. In reality, it was there all along but your subconscious mind has now cleverly brought it to your attention.

This same process works in business as well. You have an idea for a business, go through all the processes and set it up and open the doors to customers. It is only then that your subconscious mind now brings to your attention all the other businesses doing exactly the same thing and all you can think of now is "the competition". Not a good focus to have.

Over the many years that I have been working with businesses of all sizes and at all stages in their life cycle, the one thing that I have learnt is that no two of them are exactly the same. Each one has different present strengths and future strengths (note – I do not use the term weaknesses!). It is focussing on those positive differences that can give you an edge and carve you out a marketplace of your own, no matter how many other people are doing similar things.

The One and Only

The concept of a Unique Selling Proposition has been covered extensively over the years in books, on MBA programs and by marketing experts of all shapes and sizes, but it is one of those phrases that could be easily dismissed as "marketing speak" by the SME business, without realising what a valuable tool it can be. So how unique do you need to be?

The really exciting development in the world of business, that has only really come into its own since the internet search engines made it possible to quickly locate the smallest and most obscure product or service anywhere in the world at the click of a mouse, is the Niche Business.

Niche businesses can now thrive in a global marketplace. All of a sudden, geographical location is not an issue. Having a retail shop in a prime position with high footfall is no longer necessary.

When searching for a product or service, it is no longer part of our criteria that they are located around the corner. We can now order anything and have the expectation that it will arrive at our door the following day. The customer is king and will go wherever they can to get what they need, when they need it.

All of a sudden, it doesn't matter what size of business you are, or where you are located. The levelling factor is that every website is viewed on the same size of screen in the same frame. What you do in that space is up to you. You can now go head to head with any other business. Exciting times! That is why it is really important to understand those things that make you special; the things that bring your customers back again and again; the reasons they choose you and not a similar business around the corner. What is your USP? Sometimes it can be such a tiny thing that it could be easily dismissed.

For example, it could be your positive attitude, the way you serve customers; how you make them feel and how you add value to your relationship with them by sharing your knowledge and advice. There are many occasions where you might not be the closest, the most convenient or even the cheapest, but your customers still choose to do business with you, rather than another business closer to them, because of something as small as that. Don't underestimate this!

One of my clients, Robbie Williams (not the pop star!), of Impact Data Solutions, has successfully set up a rapidly growing data cabling company. He has achieved a turnover of near to £1 million in his first year and is on target to double that in year two with some impressive blue chip clients. What's his USP? It's him! His attitude and his ethics in the industry, that's what makes a hugely successful business. Never underestimate the difference you make.

It might BE your connections, if you are an avid networker and that you know who to go to in order to get something done. It might be your knowledge and the advice that you provide to your customers.

Knowledge can be a great differentiator, especially if you package and leverage it. By doing so, you demonstrate your status as an expert in your field rather than just another supplier. People will also gravitate to where they get the most value.

Whatever the reason that people choose you, it is important that you know what it is. People buy people before they buy products.

I've seen companies who are winning business purely because of the values that they lead with. It could be your proposition, it could be the way you've packaged your way in your industry, slightly different to competitors, looking at how you position yourself, or it might be your business model. Just take a look at all these different areas.

Be aware that if you are the main or only reason that people buy from your company, it is going to make an exit strategy a lot more difficult in the future, and will influence the strategy you choose in moving forward.

Discovering your USP

Sometime we are too close to our business to be objective, so if you really want to find out the real reason that people are attracted to do business with you (as distinct from what you think it is), you need to ask other people some open questions. This will help you to separate facts from feelings.

For example, you could:

- Add a customer feedback facility on your website Send out a post transaction email inviting feedback
- Write a personal letter asking "How was it for you?"
- Ask your staff to report what customers say Follow up on customers who have not returned for some time. "Was it something I said?"
- Ask friends and family how they view your business from the outside
- Start a mystery shopper programme

The closer you are to the sharp end of your business, the more you will be aware of what customers are saying, the problems that they are encountering, and the things that would make the biggest difference to them right now. This is invaluable information as it could be used to make in-flight course corrections to your business model.

Change is happening around us minute by minute. Those businesses that are really successful, despite what is happening around them in the marketplace, are probably very different to what they were a year ago. By listening and adapting, they are in a constant state of reinvention in order to keep their offering absolutely relevant to the moment.

There are plenty of examples of companies who have had their finger on the pulse of their customers' needs and have successfully adapted their business model to meet their needs.

Look at the way that Dell totally changed their fortunes by listening and making a comparatively tiny shift in their business model. In common with other computer manufacturers, their route to market was through the high street shops and out of town superstores. A very competitive environment.

So rather than stacking them high and having to sell them cheap to compete, they reinvented themselves as a direct to consumer manufacturer. This gave them an immediate advantage.

The customer paid them up front. They were the retailer and so had that added margin; and they built to order – so no warehouses full of stock that was quickly going out of date. This simple change transformed their fortunes and gave them a massive advantage in the marketplace. It became their USP.

So your unique selling proposition might be just a shift in business model, it might be a shift in the way you market, it could be your brand in the marketplace, it could be the product itself, or it could be the service. Just understand what makes you different and write it down!

Market Space

Moving on now to the next category in our **Strategy on a Page**™ diagram, Market Space. In America, they use the term "Sandbox" to describe the space you operate in, a phrase that immediately catapults you back to those carefree days in primary school. The sandbox was indeed a little world of its own that you played in with buckets and spades. But everything always stayed inside it. You didn't want to get sand on the floor if you knew what was good for you! So, what is your sandbox? What is your Market Space?

It is really important that you are able to clearly define this because it is something that your customers need to know. They need to know where your business is positioned and what its strengths are.

For example;
- are you a local business, a national business, or an international business?
- Are you a small business, a mid sized or large? Are you only in the online space, or do you have premises?
- What sector of the market do you serve?
- Do you only serve the trade, or are you open to everyone?
- Are you a niche business?
- What is your Market Space?

We have to define what area we're operating in because that will actually limit and define our strategy. By defining the industry we are in, it will help us define our customers and help us define our market space. It will also give us clarity for a strategy around market penetration. You need to know your sandbox.

A lack of clarity in this vital area makes for a weak offering in the marketplace.

If you are not quite sure who you are and who your ideal customer is, how can you expect them to know if you are the right business for them? Be sure of who you are, where you operate, where you add the most value and who would benefit the most from what you do.

Niche Markets

Earlier on, I mentioned Niching. It could be argued that this term has been overused, but it has also not been fully understood. Many businesses straddle a number of different niche markets but fail to capitalise on them because they lump them all together and have one offering to suit all. The great thing about true niche marketing is that it is no-cost, or at worst, low-cost, if it is done correctly. As I said earlier, those businesses that truly understand the power of niches and are prepared to devote the time to each one they serve, will give themselves a real edge. With niches, you can play in more than one sandbox!

With a company that has a number of different divisions, this might well be the case. If so, you may need to have a different Strategy on a Page™ for each one. This is the key importance for Market Space on the page; it defines the PAGE! If you are in a different market space then you need a different page, as your strategy and BGIs will be different.

It is really important to completely understand the niche or niches that you play in and understand what market space you operate in. The more defined you get this, the clearer your strategy will be.

There is a great temptation for entrepreneurs to be easily distracted and to go off chasing shiny pennies just because they are there. Never mind that it wasn't part of the strategy, or that it is not in our core market- place, it's an opportunity! And off they go. Having an entrepreneurial mindset is a great gift but without the discipline of a clear strategy and a focus on doing what it takes to achieve it, success will always be elusive.

Within my own organisation, BGI, I have three very distinct and different divisions, and each one occupies a different market space. I have DLD Private, which is my consulting business and where I do one-to-one consulting with clients from all over the world, based out of London. I deal with companies and divisions that are £10m - £100m and, as a result of that, it has a very specific strategy around it.

Next, I have deri.live, which manages my speaking business. I speak on strategy but I also draw from my experiences as a mountaineer and extreme sportsman to inspire a spirit of adventure in wider genres and talk on flow, high performance and life design. Naturally, I have a different strategy around this as it is another sandbox.

However, I do also speak internationally so immediately my strategy is different for that. I also work though a speaking manager and agent so I have a different page to accommodate this side of the business and the page is owned by the agent, not me.

In addition to this, I have BGI CORE, which is where this book sits within my business. This company is focused on making strategy accessible, which includes the creation of Software, Content and our flagship accelerator and scale up products. So this is a completely different market space and a very different strategy to go with it, all contained on a different page.

So you can see within BGI Group we have three pages already. How many pages do you have?

Market space will help you define this. What I find in a lot of companies and a lot of entrepreneurs is they are running multiple companies under one banner and it should be split out because they don't have any clarity or visibility across those companies.

In a recent example of a company I came in and dealt with, he had four companies operating under one. It looked like he was making profit, but we couldn't tell because all of his numbers and all of his revenues were flowing in under one company.

When we actually split them all out properly, what became very clear was that one company was making money, and one company was haemorrhaging money because it was a new start-up. Another of the company's companies was losing money and the other one was a bit of a question mark. Splitting them out, we were able to make strategic choices quickly rather than just have money being diverted to the wrong places.

Promise

Finally, we have come to promise. This is probably one of my favourite parts of the page because if we get this right, it could also be an important part of your USP.

Promise is crucial. It is actually what drives our customers to purchase from us and what makes us different from our competitors.

Surprisingly, whilst many of the big companies understand this and use it to great advantage, it is not as common as it should be.

Do you remember, some years ago, two of the big car hire companies were going head to head for market share? Hertz, because of its size and global reach, made the bold claim, "We are number one". Avis countered that by using the slogan, "We are number two, we try harder." Clever positioning and a great promise of good customer service.

A good promise is a very powerful thing, especially if your competitors don't have one, but it needs to be expressly spelt out, not just implied.

In reality, we create expectations with our customers that we will deliver in a particular way or in a particular time frame.

For example, Dominos Pizza had a commercial campaign in the 1980s and early 1990s which promised, "30 minutes or it's free". This was a powerful promise that helped them to gain market share. This was discontinued in 1993 because of too many accidents caused by hurried delivery drivers. Shame. It was a great promise.

What is it that you do anyway that you could formalise into a company promise? Your website up and running in 48 hours, or your money back? When speed is important to a customer with a new business, this could be a powerful offering. In reality that might be your normal turn around time, but by turning it into a promise, it becomes a differentiator and a reason to buy from you.

Company Promise

A well communicated company promise is as good as a contract, so you have to deliver, or take the consequences you have included in the promise. Will you deliver each and every time? Probably not. Life gets in the way, but if you cheerfully accept the consequences, you have strengthened your customer relationship, not detracted from it. We are all human and all make mistakes. Doing so with grace makes the promise, in a perverse way, more powerful.

Sometimes we make promises without realising it. We create expectations, even though we might have not meant to. Keeping faith with customers and meeting or exceeding their expectations can be made a promise.

It used to be the case that most business was done on a handshake. There was a clear understanding by both parties as to the nature of what was agreed and all that was required between two people of good faith was a handshake. It was a simple promise that, once made, was kept. It makes you nostalgic to even think about it!

In my own businesses, we offer a clear promise on all our products – for instance in our scale up programme we guarantee 10X ROI on your investment with us measured provided you do the work and execute. That's the promise.

If I cannot deliver huge value to people and I go the extra mile to delight my customers, then people shouldn't pay me. That's the confidence I have in my product and my service. And I have given money back – once to a celebrity as she really wasn't going to execute– and I will continue to do so if that's necessary. So think about what promise you're making to your customers.

Now it is easy to get carried away with this and over promise. When you do that, you are leaving yourself vulnerable to a fall. The secret is always to under promise and over deliver. But when you do make a clear and unambiguous promise, then you need to stick by it, and be in a position to take the consequences if you don't.

Promises and Consequences

I was once working for a large multinational which was the world leader in its particular field. Because of its size and position in the marketplace, quality was taken very seriously. In the unlikely event that something was not up to scratch or there were any quibbles whatsoever, we would immediately fix it. This was our clear promise and we stood by it.

However, there was one particular contract with a very, very large client where a previously undiscovered deficiency in one of our products unexpectedly came to light. This issue was so large that it would have had a multimillion pound negative impact on our client unless we acted very quickly. In a situation like this, speed is everything.

What became clear very quickly was the strength of the CEO and the power of our promise, because although we didn't actually quite know who was at fault at this point, the CEO stepped in and we replaced the product within two weeks. It was a direct cost to us of some £800,000.

Now, it later turned out that although part of the problem was down to us, a part of the problem was the responsibility of the client. However, without quibbling, and despite the cost, we stuck by our promise.

By stepping up, owning the problem and sticking to our promises, we delivered fully on that job. The result was that because we did so and kept our reputation intact, that client relationship grew considerably, as did the business they placed with us.

You might not yet be a multinational, but the promises you make are equally important, as are the repercussions for not keeping them. In all market- places, your reputation is the most precious thing you have.

Your promise is your reputation. Break it at your peril! So if you now have clarity on Promise, complete the last of the three boxes in this section. Now, in combination with vision, values and purpose you will have all the foundations in place that you need to start to map your strategy.

So are you ready for the next step?
Then turn the page......

Key Points

- Ask yourself the following questions:

- What is your USP? What makes you special? Your story, Your technology?

- Are you in a niche?
Identify exactly where your market space is and who your clients are

- What's your company guarantee or what promise do you give to all of your customers?

Chapter Seven

Foundations of Strategy

S o far, on our Strategy on a PageTM Journey, we have looked at Purpose, Vision and Values. Next, we looked in detail at the trio of Unique Selling Proposition, Market Space and Company Promise. When you then have clarity on all of these essential building blocks, you will have the foundations on which to build your strategy. Without these foundations, like missing any part of the foundations of a castle, your empire, as it grows, is much more likely to crumble or indeed not get off the ground at all. Now it's time for strategy itself! "At last!" I hear you cry....

A note of Caution. Please don't be tempted to speed read this book from end to end without taking the necessary action at the end of each chapter. I know that you didn't get where you are today without knowing a lot of this stuff and I know how tempting it is to blithely read through the book in search of any hidden gems or a silver bullet. Well I am telling you now, there isn't one. If you do that, you will be missing the point entirely. This is a book about action, not just knowledge about what strategy means.

The earlier chapters have been deliberately written to help you to put into your own words your own vision, your own purpose and your own values. You absolutely need to know this before moving on and that means you need to have written it down.

0 It is not enough to say, "I've got it in my head." The faintest of ink is better than the strongest of memory! You will find it invaluable to have that piece of paper beside you now as you read on so that you can glance at it and apply it to what we are about to cover.

"Creativity without strategy is called 'art'. Creativity with strategy is called 'advertising'."

Now, if you look once again at the **Strategy on a Page**™ diagram, you will see a vertical dotted line separating the first third of the diagram from the part we are now entering.
The line separates the foundations of who you are and what you stand for from the planning, direction and actions which we are about to work on.

We are about to cross the line into the area that many businesses have the most difficulty with – and I don't just mean SMEs! You would be surprised at how many larger businesses have grown without quite knowing why or how, which is fine until they

meet a major challenge or a shift in their marketplace. Without the firm foundation of all of the elements we are covering here, it is then that they are at their most vulnerable.

The world of business is littered with an elephant's graveyard of companies where a simple thing tripped them up. I only have to mention the name of Gerald Ratner.

Cautionary Tale

Gerald Ratner is a British businessman and was formerly chief executive of the major British jewelery company Ratner's Group (now the Signet Group). He based his philosophy of business on his experiences as a boy in Petticoat Lane Market where he observed that "the people who shouted the loudest and appeared to give the best offers sold the most."

With this philosophy, he shocked the staid world of the jewellery trade by displaying fluorescent orange posters advertising cut price bargains and by offering low price ranges. The public took to this new approach and the business thrived until a fateful day in 1991 when he made a now famous speech to the Institute of Directors.

During the speech, he commented: "We also do cut-glass sherry decanters complete with six glasses on a silver-plated tray that your butler can serve you drinks on, all for £4.95. People say, "How can you sell this for such a low price?" I say, "because it's total crap."

He compounded this by going on to remark that some of the earrings were "cheaper than an M&S prawn sandwich but probably wouldn't last as long." Ratner's comments have become textbook examples of the folly of making fun of, and showing contempt to, customers. In the furore that ensued, customers exacted their revenge by staying away from Ratner's shops. After the speech, the value of Ratner's Group plummeted by around £500 million, which very nearly resulted in the firm's collapse. Ratner resigned in November 1992, and the group changed its name to Signet Group in September 1993.

Today, Ratner's speech is still famous in the corporate world as an example of the value of branding and image over quality. But there are other lessons to draw from it as well.

So, how clear are you again on your Purpose, Vision and Values?

Time frame

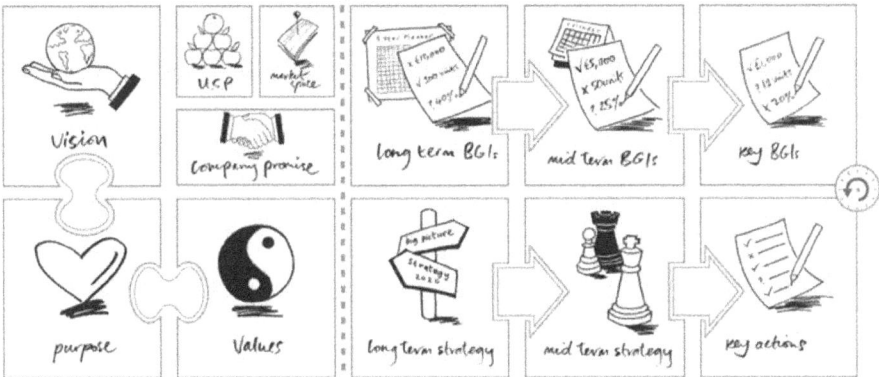

Take a look at the first three boxes on the bottom half of the Strategy on a Page™ diagram, to the right of the vertical dotted line.

Long Term Strategy (the next 12 months)
Medium Term Strategy (the next quarter)
Short Term Strategy (the next month)

Now, we touched on timescales briefly in an earlier chapter, but now is the time to really understand what Short, Medium and Long Term really means for you and your business. I cannot emphasise enough how important it is to understand this and get it right.

Before you get defensive and explain that your industry is different, the reality is that all industries have business cycles and market trends that are unique to them. Layer on top of that the different dynamics related to the size of any individual

business plus whether it is a new or established enterprise, and you see a myriad of variables. Some industries are stable and predictable, others are more dynamic and responsive.

With larger companies in a stable marketplace, long term can mean five to ten years. With some of the digital media companies I'm working with, typically the long term is just over a year, or sometimes two years at the most because the dynamic in the marketplace is changing so fast.

To go beyond one to two years in the digital media world would be futile because by the time we've reached a year or six months, the landscape has probably changed.

In addition, there are also cultural dimensions to this, both national culture as well as the corporate culture of the organisation itself. As we said earlier, some countries, like Japan, consider long term to mean anything up to one hundred years.

With so many variables, this is the reason that so many people are put off from engaging with the strategy process.

But if you remember, I did say that strategy IS simple. So simple that it can fit on one page! So before your eyes glaze off with too many possibilities, let us provide you with an easy way of applying this stuff to your business, the size it is right now, and the real world it occupies.

So, what do time frames mean to you?

Ask yourself these questions;

- How fast is your industry moving?
- How often do dramatic changes or market forces create the need to change course?
- How predictable are those changes in your marketplace?
- What can you learn by looking at the market leaders in your marketplace?
- What is it that drives change with your customers?
- What time frame feels right for you where you could plan ahead with confidence?

The way we all perceive time will be different and largely influenced by the pace of life that we lead. When we are very young and count down the days to the start of a holiday by the number of "sleeps", time just seems to drag. Later on, as the world of business engulfs us, it seems that no sooner have we started the week than Friday is upon us. Yes, and the policemen seem to be getting younger as well!

Time is our most precious possession, which is why we are taking it so seriously here. We can take back control of time if we have a clear idea of what needs to be done, and by when, in order for us to stay on track and achieve those bigger goals that seem just over the horizonat the moment.

Now, typically in 95% of the businesses that I work with, long term strategy means one year Medium term is one quarter and short term is a month.

Bear in mind that these are the time frames that you, or your board or shareholders, will be holding yourself to account by, and taking stock of progress in

Deadlines cause things to happen and review dates to take stock of what has actually happened are absolutely essential.

These milestones are essential to avoid drifting.

If you are a start-up business, for you the Long Term may well be one quarter, medium-term being a month and short-term being a week because there are so many dynamics and so much going on.

If you are in any doubt or unsure, go with one year, one quarter and one month and get on with it, but don't procrastinate! You can change time frames later if they don't work for you. Typically, I look my clients in the eye and say, "We are going to map Long Term Strategy now and you need to be comfortable with it so without thinking, and I need an answer in five seconds tops, what does long term mean to you? Go!"

Your gut reaction is usually the right answer – so decide! As the leader of your business, one of the ualities you will need is to have a wide field of vision and thus the ability to be able to stand back, at regular intervals, and take in the bigger picture.

This is not easy if the day-to-day operational requirements of the business are urgent and demanding. I once worked with a company in the financial services industry which comes under my definition of a stable industry, and one where a five year Long Term Strategy would be considered the norm.

However, the Managing Director was so engulfed in the day-to-day and week-by-week demands of the business that he found it difficult to map out the next two weeks. In these circumstances, we have to reduce his timeline to 1 month

segments because he was so much in the 'now'. What I am saying is that there are no hard and fast rules to this because everyone is different. You will need to bear this in mind when getting 'buy-in' from the rest of the team.

Business Growth Indicators

Now, before moving on, I would like to draw your attention to the three boxes on the Strategy on a Page™ diagram, directly above the Long Term, Medium and Short Term. As you will see, there is a vertical alignment for each of the strategies to a corresponding Business Growth Indicator.

These will hold you accountable, give you a mirror to hold up to your business, and give you the means to measure your progress. The key point is that whatever strategy is going on and whatever time frame you choose, the Business Growth Indicators are the measure to ensure that you achieve the strategy you set out. So just be aware of that for the next chapter.

The point is doing the big things all the time. So, the themes horizontally are typically all the major areas of the business. Don't forget that the definition of strategy is "a plan for obtaining a major result". So all of these strategicobjectives here are major results, which means that they are the major elements of your business.

The other thing to consider here is the horizontal alignment with strategy. You will see there are five boxes in strategy. These represent the five core strategic actions running through the company.

Every now and again, a company adds one or takes one away, but typically we always end up back with five and that's the point.

You can keep focused on five core strategic priorities at any one point in time.

If it starts going beyond that, you're probably getting tactical, or you probably need multiple pages because you've got a more complex business.

"However beautiful the strategy, you should occasionally look at the results."

Winston Churchill

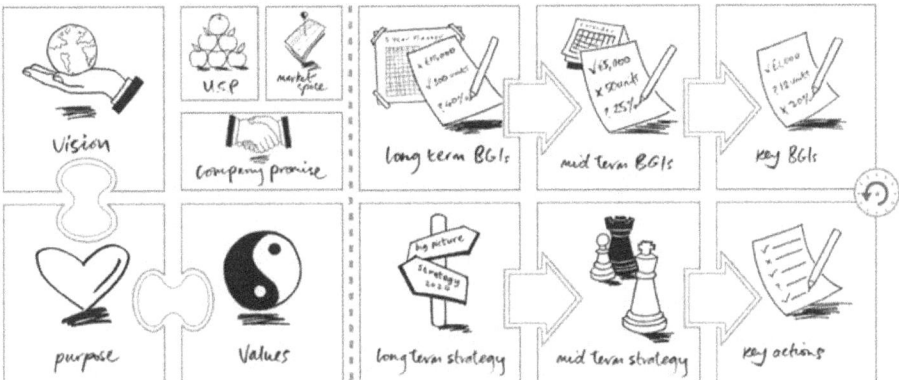

The Foundations of Strategy

Whenever I work inside a business and discuss strategy with the management team or the directors, I find that the different people tend to focus on the aspect of strategy that they feel most comfortable with.

For example, if the CEO has a sales background then, unsurprisingly, the sales element of strategy is likely to be the most robust. Conversely, if their background is financial that focus is most likely to shine through. But for strategy to really work, it has to be well balanced across all areas of the business, not just the ones on which you feel strongest.

This is why it's key to have a balance across all major strategies in the business, to create a really solid foundation for moving forward. Without solid foundations, any structure you build on top of them is likely to crumble.

The five core strategic objectives in all businesses are:

Marketing, Sales, Operations, Talent and Finance

I am not saying that your business will look like that to you right now. There may be a subtle difference. For example, with some businesses that I work with, marketing is not so relevant, because it is more of a direct sales organisation.

With other businesses, there may be no need for an HR department because everything's outsourced or delivered through freelancers. In this case, I would argue that whether they are directly employed or not, is not the point as you are still working through people to achieve your objectives and you need to track and measure this in the same way as everything else.

So, don't get hung up with these five; they are just a suggestion of the key place holders to start you thinking about what these major categories are in your own business. In my experience, five is about the right number. But before we look at this in more detail, I have an important exercise for you first: the Eight Box S.W.O.T. Analysis.

The Eight Box S.W.O.T. Analysis

	Strengths	Weaknesses
Opportunities	Wealth Strategy	Development Strategy
Threats	Toughen Up Strategy	Critical Strategy

Now, the S.W.O.T. Analysis is one of the most commonly used strategic tools in the world and most of the time, it is used very badly. The reason is that most people believe that all you need to do once you have used it, is to convert your weaknesses to strengths, and your threats into opportunities and job done, off to the pub. Well no, it doesn't work that way.

Instead, if we have identified weaknesses, then you should look to fix them, either by bringing in someone to delegate that task to, or outsource it entirely. This will free you up to focus your total attentions on building upon your strengths and capitalising upon the opportunities in the market space.

If there is nobody better in the company at doing what you do best, then absolutely, you should do more of it and less of the things that stop you from being at your most productive.

To start this exercise, you will need more space than is available on the diagram to follow, so find some sheets of paper or a pad, and create one page each for Strengths, Weaknesses, Opportunities and Threats.

Strengths and weaknesses are internal to the company, and opportunities and threats are external.

Then you will need to make a larger version of the diagram on one sheet, and transfer the key points from the other sheets into the appropriate boxes.

Either do this on your own or, if you're working in a slightly bigger company, bring in some of your senior management team to do this exercise with you so you get a more rounded approach. It is really important to get a full inventory of where you're at right now.

Of course, this is just a snapshot of where you are right now, and hopefully, if you do this exercise in six months' time, it should be subtly different.

Are you in the Zone?

You will notice on the S.W.O.T. diagram that there are four boxes in the middle.

- **Where your weaknesses meet your threats, that is your Critical Strategy.**
- **Where your strengths meet your opportunities, that is your Wealth Strategy.**
- **Where your weaknesses meet your opportunities, that's the Development Strategy.**
- **Where your strengths meet your threats, that is the Toughen up Strategy.**

So, what does this mean in practice?

What we're looking to do is to mirror and match across and understand where strengths meet weaknesses.

For instance, finance is typically coming out as a weakness. This might manifest itself in limited cash flow or cash reserves available, or it might be bad credit control.

Typically, a lot of weaknesses sit in the financial arena and very often the external threats to a company happen when you've run out of money or a competitor attacks and you do not have the money to invest.

A threat is potentially a move by a competitor or a launch of something new in the marketplace, potentially an innovation, and now due to your limited fiscal ability you can't capitalise in the marketplace and that's shown in the Critical Strategy.

So, the learning point from that is that we really need to harden up our finances and really take control of our cash control, raise capital or build cash reserves. This will be identified as a strategic priority.

126

How was it for you?

Conversely, if you're really strong in that area, and if your current clients, your relationships and your customer service are all really strong, there's a huge opportunity to up-sell, cross-sell and capitalise on additional products within your current customer portfolio. That's where your Wealth Strategy lies.

So, going off just chasing loads of new customers when you haven't fully capitalised on the ones you've got in front of you would be foolhardy. I see this all the time! I find a lot of people are sitting on a potential wealth which they're not fully aware of. This would certainly be a strategic priority because of what is typically known as "low-hanging fruit".

It is important that you don't skip this exercise and keep on reading. So can I now invite you to STOP, get some sheets of paper and do your S.W.O.T. Straight away. Don't worry, this will still be here when you get back, and it will then mean a lot more as a result.

GET S.W.O.T.ting!!!

I hope you found that to be a helpful exercise. I have found it one of the quickest ways to give a quick snapshot of where you're at in your business right now.

You might want to explore other tools for your business as well. For example, you could use the balanced score card methodologies or K-T analysis, or any number of other strategic tools. Whatever you're used to, or whatever is valid to you, never forget that these tools only work if you use them regularly and make good use of the insights they will provide – and then act on them! More info on the www.strategyonapage.biz website.

Mapping your Strategy

You are now at the point where you can take all the elements you have created so far and start entering them onto your Strategy on a Page™ sheet.

Take all of your "Off the Page" notes you have been making, such as the S.W.O.T. Analysis, and prepare to copy the main conclusions "Onto the Page", your Strategy on a Page™ sheet or software.

You will also want to go back and have the five CoreDrivers of your business that you identified earlier, readily to hand. Each of these will be represented on one of the five lines in each of the three strategy boxes on the bottom row of the sheet.

Typically, when you start entering your strategies onto the Page, you start from right to left. You start with your Key Actions for right now, your Strategic Drivers for the quarter, and then your Core strategy for the next year (if that is the time frame you have chosen).

Then from left to right, you transfer core strategies which flow from your Purpose, Vision and Values, along with your Unique Proposition, Defined Market Space and your Company Promise.

You'll be amazed how powerful this suddenly becomes when you see it all together on one piece of paper. And if you find it powerful, just imagine how it will have the power to give focus and direction to the people around you as well.

The Key Elements to your Strategy?

If we're looking at a strategy to exit yourself from the business, then layering an organisational structure which is self-managing is going to be key in the long- term, whereas in the medium-term you might just need to be putting in a management structure.

If a key element of your vision is brand, then this will need to be reflected in your marketing strategy and also be a big part of your Key Actions for right now.

Maybe it is more than that and you want to be one of the well recognised brands in your industry in five years' time and winning industry national awards. If that is the case, then what will need to be achieved in the year ahead to move towards that goal?

More importantly, what needs to be done this month to really starting to establishing your brand? Everything comes back to how you need to be acting on it now. If it's strategically important and you've identified it as a major part of your strategy, you should be working on it every single month.

If you want to be known for amazing customer service and delighting your customers, then this will need to be reflected in your operational strategy.

How could you do this? Maybe a new Customer Relationship Management system; maybe upgrading your operational systems. But whatever it means to you, and based on what you have identified in the S.W.O.T. Analysis, now is the time

to plan to bridge the gap between where you are today, and where you need to be in the future.

Strategy is simply the bridge between those two points, a plan, nothing more complicated than that!

Let's take a look at the Five Core Areas of strategy and see where you might sit in each one.

Let's use Finance as another example as it is one of the Five Core Strategies for every business. Again, you may well have identified some key action points in this area from your S.W.O.T. Analysis. So, what is it that you need to achieve? Is your focus to sell off the company, or part of the company? Are you looking to make an exit? You might have a particular figure for the value of the business in mind, say three million in five years' time driven through a series of small acquisitions and building on organic growth. That's a financial strategy.

To achieve it might require putting in cash reserves through the business. Cash reserves may be key to you raising capital for the next element of the business. It might be putting in a robust financial system if you are currently not getting what you want. Or putting in a management information system so you're actually extracting data you need to make decisions.

It could be hiring the next financial person, it could be getting a bookkeeper, it could be changing your accountant, it could be getting in a financial director or a financial controller. There are many different strategies around finance, but that doesn't mean it needs to be complicated.

All you are looking to do is to bridge between where you are now and where you need to be and what needs to happen to make that so. That will be your strategy for finance.

Operations

Now, obviously Operations and what it encompasses means different things in different industries. If you are in manufacturing, then your strategy in this area might be focused on driving efficiencies through the business, or investing in new processes or new technology.

If you are in more of a service based industry, it could be based around ways that your Customer Relationship Management systems help to increase the lifetime value of a customer, or are able to deliver companion products or services to add on to what they traditionally buy from you. It might mean increasing the resources to offer a more personal service to your customers.

So in your world, Operations might not be one of the Five Core Strategies. You might want to call it Service, for example. Again, this does not need to be complicated. Where are you now with this, and where do you need to be? What will it take to bridge that gap? That will be your strategy.

Marketing

If the way you are currently marketing your business is the same as it was 12 months ago then, even if you haven't changed, the world has changed around you, and so have your customers. There is no one area that is more susceptible to change than the whole area of Marketing.

It may well be that you have just woken up to the world of social media and AI and you need to find a seven- year-old to explain it to you. Certainly there is much happening in that space and some businesses have gained much by positioning themselves there.

Are you looking at rebranding and, if so, was this an emotional decision or one based on an in-depth look at how you are positioned and perceived in your marketplace?

Do you need some reliable data on which to base decisions as to which direction to take your marketing?

Do you need to draw on some expert analysis?

Are you measuring the results generated by your online presence? Do you know what the trends are?

Do you know how to influence them? Marketing can be a complex subject if you let it.

Fortunately, as the leader of your business, you don't need to be an expert. All you need to be able to do is to ask the right questions, and then act on the answers.

As long as you track and measure everything, you will quickly know what works and what doesn't. You will know what the trends are and what needs to be addressed. You can then make the right things happen.

As there may be a number of different strands to your marketing, there is no reason why you cannot have additional sheets on this to support your main Strategy on a PageTM, but keep that page as simple as you can.
Ask yourself, where are you now? Where do you need
to be? What will it take to bridge that gap? Keep it simple!
But powerful

"The aim of marketing is to know and understand
the customer so well that the product or service sells itself."
Sales

In my experience, there is often very little wrong with a business that a few extra customers couldn't put right. Yet so many businesses think of sales as a reactive, rather than a proactive function. It is one thing to make a sale when someone walks in the door, but another one entirely to get them to walk through the door (or virtual door) in the first place.

Having a sales pipeline, a sales funnel and knowing your conversion ratios from suspect to prospect to customer is the only way you will be able to be in charge of this vital element of your business.

What do you need to do to positively influence sales? Do you need to hire and train a new sales person?

Do you have a robust process in place to evaluate potential employees and ensure they have all the appropriate skills, values and qualities you need?

How will you be measuring what they do? Do you have a way of seeing the relationship between calls, contacts, appointments, presentations and sales?

Can you extract from those ratios where a salesperson's strengths and weaknesses are? How good is your organisation at managing the sales process?

Are you where you need to be, or do you need to make changes? What is it going to take in the next month to make a difference? How will you know if you have?

Human Resources

Looking at the big picture of which direction you want to move your business towards, what are the implications for your people, your contractors, your freelancers, your employees, associates or partners?

Are you involved in succession planning?

Do you need to put in place new people to take over the aspects of the business you are currently doing yourself?

Have you grown to a point that you now need an HR department to take some of that administrative burden off you or others?

Are your HR systems delivering to the needs of the business? Do you need to outsource your HR function?

Look at where you are now, and where you need to be. What needs to happen? Add it to your Strategy on a Page™.

"Good management is the art of making problems so interesting and their solutions so constructive that everyone wants to get to work and deal with them."

Paul Hawken

Summary of Chapter Seven

Take stock of your progress

Well, you have come a long way in this chapter. If you have been doing all the exercises and writing down the insights and the learning points you have had, you should be a lot clearer on what your Strategy on a PageTM is starting to look like.

If you have been cheating and reading ahead and not doing your homework, then all you will have are a few superficial ideas and little more. This book is all about learning through doing. So, no cheating please!

You have looked in depth at purpose, vision and values; your unique selling proposition; the market space you operate in; and the promise you give your customers. It is knowledge based on those core fundamentals in your business that will allow you to drive the strategy necessary to move you forward to the next level.

You should now have identified the five elements of strategy appropriate to your business and will have

mapped out where you need to be in the Long Term and what you need to be doing this month to ensure that happens.

Once you have your five core strategies in the month, quarter and in the year, you should now identify what the top one is.

There's usually one strategy which is most important of all and the one that's usually not being done. It could be within your Critical Strategy or your weak area. Identify it and focus on it.

S.W.O.T.

You've also done an exercise off the page, to help you gain clarity on your Strengths, Weaknesses, Opportunities and Threats, and what you can learn from this and apply it to your strategy moving forward.

You will have seen the strategies for opportunity and threat, and you now understand how to map that back into the business. So you are making the bridge.

Remember, strategy is the bridge between the big picture of where you want to be and where you are now. It provides the framework to move towards those objectives step-by-step every single month, piece by piece, and by doing so, ensures that the major core strategies for the business are achieved.

But you are not quite there yet. You will have noticed that there are three boxes on your sheet that are still empty. Your Business Growth Indicators. These are the tools you will use to effectively measure the strategy and your progress.

It's all very well saying you're going to do something, but how do you know it has actually been done, and how do you measure the success over time? These are business growth indicators, and that's the next chapter. Following that, you go into the all panel full accountability section, and this is where the magic starts to happen.

It's all very well spending all this time on strategy but if you don't actually do it and if you don't hold yourself accountable, all of this will be wasted.

Study - Getting clarity on your core purpose

One of the things that gives me the most psychic reward in my own business is working with people who are passionate about what they do and are really tuned in to providing the best possible service to their customers. But sometimes that enthusiasm to over deliver can move a business away from its core purpose and objectives.

Recently, I had the pleasure of working with two very passionate and talented guys and their company, Greedy Media. Rob and Justin are joint MDs and between them have considerable experience in the whole world of video production. One was a producer, the other a director, so they really knew their subject.

They are running a very successful business and are really busy. The reason that they wanted to work with me was to take it to the next level.

Because they were really tuned in and responsive to the needs of their clients, the business had grown from being just focused on video production and had developed into a full digital agency. This was a direction that many other businesses

in their market sector had taken, and by developing in this way they were able to offer a far wider range of services to their customers.

When we started to work of their Strategy on a Page™ and looked at the purpose, vision and values pieces of the company, it became clear that they were trying to be something that they were not. The move to broaden their offering into a digital agency had, in fact, moved them away from their true passion, which was video production.

To help give them clarity, we did the Eight Box S.W.O.T. Analysis. From this, it became clear that there was a massive opportunity in the market for them to just be who they are, and to focus on that passion.

For them, as specialist digital video producers, the potential for them was huge and to move into other areas which were not their passion was distracting them from this purpose.

When we looked at other digital agencies in the marketplace, it became clear that most of them did not have an in-house capability for video production, and needed to outsource this service. Rather than competing with them and trying to be a digital agency themselves, why not turn them into customers? When we started the map strategy, a whole different direction emerged for them to be the absolute specialists for all the digital agencies out there.

With this subtle shift of strategy, we were able to refocus them back onto what they're passionate about, where they add the most value.

On their S.W.O.T. Analysis, it placed them at the point where their strengths are and also where the opportunities are in the marketplace, so it's totally in their Wealth Strategy. As a result, their strategy is now robust, their plans for the next three to five years are clear and their execution in the month is absolutely spot on. Their growth in the last four months alone is phenomenal and now we're trying to control that growth moving forward. A fantastic position to be in.

When you get this clarity, and when you're aligned to your purpose and your vision, this is where the power and the magic happens. Strategy is not rocket science and in retrospect and in hindsight, it always looks simple and obvious.

The key to it is in taking the time to ask the most difficult and fundamental questions about the business that we focused on in the first half of this book

So have you allowed to be distracted from your core purpose and away from your passion?

Key Points

- If you don't have your company foundations (left side of the page) in place, your company will be unstable in growth

- Identify your time frames and then set benchmark targets for short, medium and long term strategies

- Business growth indicators will hold you accountable and hold a mirror up to your own actions

- The five core objectives in business are:
- Sales, Marketing, Operations, Finance and Human Resources
- Conduct an Eight Box S.W.O.T. Analysis to get clear on your positioning

"The things that are easy to do, are also easy not to do. That is the difference between success and failure, pennies and fortunes."

Jim Rohn

Chapter Eight
Business Growth Indicators

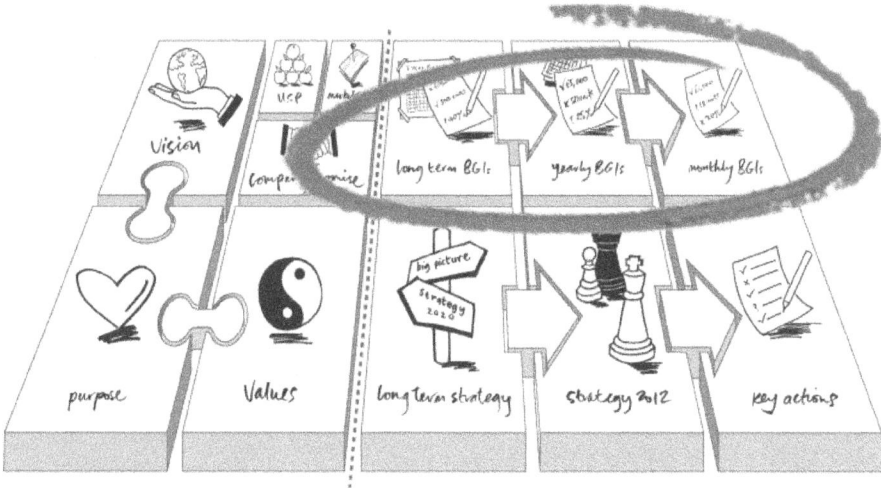

Y ou are getting tantalisingly close to completing all the sections on our Strategy on a Page™. At this point in the journey, if you have 'played the game' and completed all of the exercises, and put some serious thought into answering all the questions that have been posed, you may well be feeling good with the clarity that you are now getting on moving your business forward, based on the firm foundations of your vision, purpose and values.

You should now have a clear idea of what your focus needs to be in the next month in order to be where you need to at

the end of the year, and on track to achieve your long term goals. So let me bring you back down to earth. None of this can happen if you do not have in place a 'dashboard' of instruments for you to refer to, so that you know you are on track to achieve this. You need to have a simple way of measuring your progress. The three boxes at the top of the diagram and to the right of the dotted vertical line, are your Business Growth Indicators.

Just like the petrol gauge or the oil light in your car, they will immediately flag up when there is something that needs your attention.

What is the difference between a KPI and a BGI?

What is the difference between Key Performance Indicators (KPIs) and Business Growth Indicators (BGIs)? I tend to think of KPIs as a way of measuring individual progress or processes within the business.

You are on a higher level looking at the Strategy of the business, so I believe that Business Growth Indicators are the best way I have found to ensure that the business is indeed growing in the way that has been planned. BGIs are a way of focusing on the really important numbers because, as you know by now, strategy is the plan to achieve a major result. Notice that the key word here is 'numbers'.

I know that whenever I mention numbers at one of my Business Growth Seminars, there is an audible groan in the room. So many SMEs are driven by their passion, enthusiasm, talent and focus which uses up all their energy. They believe that if they put in enough work and delight enough customers, the numbers will happen by themselves.

Nice thought, but sorry; no!

Many SMEs stay as SMEs simply because they didn't pay enough attention to the numbers or were not looking at the right numbers in order to get answers.

Personally, I love numbers, but I do understand that it is not a core skill that everybody shares. That is why in Strategy on a Page™, we have created some easy ways of measuring the numbers for people who don't like numbers but need to see the big picture. These are our Business Growth Indicators.

Higher, Faster, Longer

As you may know, I find relaxation by climbing the odd mountain, running across the occasional desert and completing an Iron Man Challenge to pass away a weary hour. You might be forgiven into thinking that with such physical sports, numbers might be the last thing on my mind. You would be wrong. Numbers are the difference between life and death, especially when you are at 20,000 feet up and surrounded by snow.

For instance, whilst I was on Aconcagua, which is the highest mountain outside the Himalayas, one of my 10 buddies looked to be in trouble with altitude sickness. When we measured oxygen saturation, it had gone down to a really dangerous level. Thankfully, we were able to get him off the mountain quickly. If we hadn't spotted it and we hadn't been measuring the right things, it could have resulted in a real disaster on the mountain.

The numbers that I measure on a mountain are very different to the numbers I measure when I am running across the desert. I need very different indicators. If I was trying to use the same form of measurement for both, I would be getting a very different result and getting a false impression.

Measuring altitude is necessary on a mountain, but it is of no value running across a desert. In fact, the added weight to enable you to do so would be a hindrance.

What does a BGI look like?

It's the same for your business. You need to use the right indicators and measure the right things to enable you to effectively manage your particular situation. Just like an athlete, a business is a living thing and has vital signs that need monitoring. Not doing so could spell disaster.

The benefit of Strategy on a Page™, and the Business Growth Indicators, is that it enables you to proactively spot trends well in advance, and before the actual problems hit.

When we cover the subject of accountability in a later chapter, this will become very evident.

If in mountaineering terms, in desert terms and also endurance terms, measuring the numbers are indeed the difference between life and death, it is no different with your business. BUT, you have to be using the right indicators to know your vital signs!

Earlier I said that the Five Core Areas of Strategy are, by and large, almost the same for most businesses. This principle does not apply to Business Growth Indicators which can look very different depending on the business concerned. They are the numbers we need to see in the company, in the short term, medium term and long term, to track the company and ensure it is going in the right direction.

As you will see from the Strategy on a PageTM, there is a direct relationship between the three boxes on the top row and the three boxes on the bottom. The BGIs for your Long Term strategy will reflect the results of the same core

strategies in the boxes below. The same for the Strategic Drivers, and also the Key Actions for this month. Each BGI is the way of measuring one of the Core Strategies.

The important thing is that the BGIs need to cover all the elements of the company and reflect progress on achieving the Five Core Strategies in a measurable way.

Measuring the right things

What you measure will also be determined by what the final outcome is going to be. For example, if your plan is to exit the business and sell it in a few years' time, the main things that you may be measuring are revenue and profit. Typically, most SMEs look at this at the end of the year when their accountant produces the books.

If exiting is your focus, you are probably measuring revenue, sales and profitability and driving sales hard in order to exit for the biggest price in five years' time.

If that is the case, you could be measuring the wrong thing. Depending on your industry, what you need to know is a strange thing called EBITDA. This is shorthand for Earnings Before Interest, Tax, Depreciation and Amortisation.

If your eyes just glazed over, don't worry. You are not alone. It is actually a simple enough number which your accountant will be able to provide. The reason why we want to be measuring EBITDA is that if you're looking for a sale, this is the number that most professional valuers will use to arrive at the value of the business. If you are moving towards a sale, driving revenues is not always the right answer.

Whatever your long term goals are, you need to make sure you are measuring the right things to achieve them. This is why getting the right Business Growth Indicators is so important.

So how do you measure?

Obviously, some things are easier and more obvious to measure than others. There will be areas of your business where you might not immediately see an easy way of doing this, but they still need to be measured nonetheless.

Whilst you are looking for ways of doing so, it might be that it could take a longer period to do this, and this is fine. On your page, you may have a blank Business Growth Indicator for several months, even up to six months, whilst you are putting in the right systems to be able to measure it.

Measuring progress in the area of Brand Awareness, for example, might be challenging to start with but you might later find a correlation with traffic to your website or with new customer enquiries, and could use that as a BGI.

With Marketing, it might be easier. Here, you could use a measurable return on investment in order to track the progress of your activities.

The Hammock Test

Just suppose that your business was now at a point where you had decided to go to the Bahamas and put your feet up whilst the business ticked over without you. It doesn't have to be the Bahamas, of course; you could choose Bridlington instead if you prefer.

The point is that you left clear instructions to whoever was running the business in your absence to send you a monthly copy of your page. What are the figures on that page that would tell you everything you needed to know about where the business stood on that day in relation to your strategy?

What would tell you that your business is running well? You are not looking to fill the page with anything that is a nice-to-know, only the must-knows. Keep it simple.

Imagine, for example, that you were lying in that hammock and you were given your Profit and Loss accounts and your balance sheet to look at.

What could they tell you? It might be that revenues were looking good, and profitability was good. Does that mean your business is doing well?

Not necessarily, because there could be a whole lot of other things going on that would not show up on those figures. For example,

It could be revenue is looking good now because they've just nailed a big account. However, there maybe no new business in the pipeline moving forward.

It could be that some of your best customers have just left you, but you don't know it yet because it hasn't hit the balance sheet.

It could be that three of your key staff have just walked out and you're not aware of it.

Your customer service is going down the pan because the remaining staff are too maxed out and you're going to lose customers as a result of it.

All these things you don't know, and you can't measure them based on just revenue and profitability.

That's what you're trying to do with your BGIs. You want to have a full picture of the Business Growth Indicators across the business so you can sit in a hammock comfortably knowing that the business is running well or, if there are problems, you can quickly identify them, and fix them, before they have a knock-on effect.

Don't forget that all Business Growth Indicators are directly aligned to the time frame shown on the core strategies they relate to, in the boxes below them on the page. So whatever time you have identified as your strategic medium term, long term and short term or key actions, these will be directly mirrored in your Business Growth Indicators.

Setting the right timescales is a really important part of this so that they present you with meaningful milestones at intervals that give you the opportunity to make course corrections in good time, if required.

What do Business Growth Indicators look like?

They're a bit of a blend of past, present and future. You need to have a mix of what's happened, what's happening and what's going to happen within the business in number terms.

Many SMEs measure things in their business far too late for the information to be of any practical use.

For example, if all they do is rely on the end of year accounts to provide them with a snapshot of where their business is, they will probably have to wait a further six months to get this information from their accountants. By this time, so much else will have happened in the business that the information will only be of passing historic interest. That, to me, is criminal. You can't manage a business by just knowing its history.

If you do not have your finger on the pulse of your business on a month-by-month basis, then strategy is the least of your worries. You cannot drive a car wearing a blindfold. Finding out what happened six months after the end of your year is pointless because it is too late to do anything about it. That's lazy and that's not strategic. However, you do still need that information, as you will shortly see.

Knowing the past performance and the historical trends from your profit and loss and your balance sheets will show you what's actually happened, but it won't give you detailed trends of all the different factors if you haven't been measuring them up until now.

You will find that, in the Strategy on a Page™ software, we have developed a very cool way of using your historical trends and Business Growth Indicators month-by- month over a period of time as an incredibly powerful decision making tool. More on that in the next chapter when we look at Accountability.

But now, let's move from the Past into The Present

What's happening in the business right now?
How do you keep our finger on the pulse of the business?
What aspects of the business do you need to know about and be able to measure?

Let's start with your people. People in your business are both your biggest asset, and also, probably, your biggest expense. How do you measure this resource and use it as a Business Growth Indicator?

There are a number of ways to do this. Measuring the percentage of PAYE to revenue is a good indicator. It will typically flux up and down as you recruit more staff or as you lose staff, so there will be a kind of pinch point of how many people you need.

This is a great indicator for when to recruit. Typically, people recruit to fill a gap when somebody leaves.

However, if you're growing fast, it is easy to become incredibly stretched over a period of time and not realise that it was necessary to recruit to accommodate that demand.

Tracking this BGI alerts you to this and helps you to be proactive rather than reactive to keep the capacity of your staff and the business at the right level.

If your revenues are increasing, your percentage from PAYE to revenue should increase proportionately. This is not always the case, but it's a good indicator that you might need some more people.

Capacity

Another indicator in alignment to this will be capacity. It depends on what business you're in, but what does capacity look like to you? How do you know what percentage of capacity you are working to? If you're in a service industry, are your people working to full capacity? How do you know? If they are, when do you recruit?

Many businesses in the media and creative industries outsource work with freelancers, rather than employ full-time staff. Measuring revenues against the cost of outsourcing will tell you when it could be more profitable to employ more staff in-house, who tend to be cheaper than freelancers. Another important BGI to consider. Cash flow.

Another thing which is critical to manage in the present is cash flow. Everybody talks about cash flow but very few SMEs can measure it properly, particularly on a month-by-month basis. It's not rocket science, but you need to have the right systems in place to do it effectively.

- What does your cash flow look like?
- What cash reserves do you have?
- Do you have big swings in your cash flow?
- Is your business vulnerable when a negative swing occurs?
- How far ahead can you currently predict that this could happen?

So, how can you manage this if you can't predict the future? Read on!

The Future

For many companies, looking ahead into the future is a problem. There are too many imponderables, so they think, "Why make an uninformed guess?" In my experience, however, the future is not guesswork but a logical progression based on facts and trends. If you have the right Business Growth Indicators in place. it is easier than you think.

Let's look at something we can measure and understand – cash. Cash flows in, cash flows out and if you have the proper controls and systems in place, you can see trends and patterns emerge. If your financial systems have yet to catch up with your needs and are not providing you with the information you need, then you should make this one of your core strategies.

155

The one thing you can control and predict is what you spend with both your fixed and variable costs. You should be able to map that forward. In reality most people's expenditures don't vary very much, especially if you control them properly.

Sales Pipeline

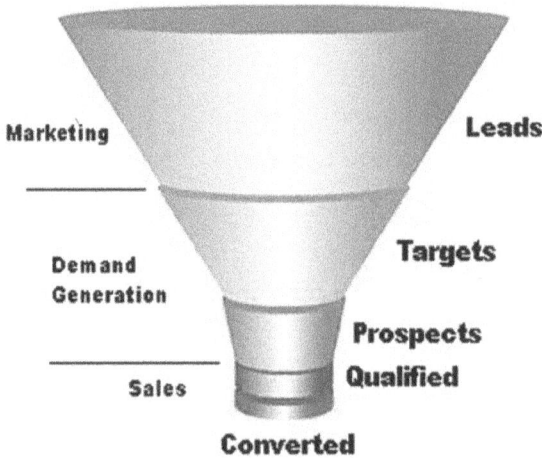

To manage your cash flow, you need to understand what is going out, and also what's coming in. How can you predict sales with all the current vagaries of the marketplace? The answer is to put in place the one thing that seems to be missing from so many businesses – the sales pipeline, or the sales funnel as it is also known.

You should know what is in your pipeline over the next one, two, three months, six months. Obviously, it will depend on what industry you're in and what you're selling and over what period of time, but the pipeline is absolutely key as it is a very powerful way of predicting your sales income. You don't need to guess your cash flow if you have a good handle on what is entering your sales funnel.

In fact, you can go back even further and look at conversion ratios for every lead that enters the funnel. If you know the number of calls it takes to speak to a prospective customer; the number of customers you need to speak to in order to secure get an appointment; and the number of presentations it takes to land a sale, then you are completely in control. To influence your sales income, all you need to do is to increase the amount of marketing activity it takes in order to get someone to talk to you in the first place. Knowing your conversion ratios is also key.

Now, don't misunderstand pipeline. A lot of people misinterpret pipeline as only the business that they've actually got signed up.

That is not the case. If the business is already on the books, it has moved out of the pipeline.

The sales pipeline needs to include all the probabilities of all future sales, what's going to come in, and when it is due to happen. All of this impacts your cash flow and will affect your planning.

One of the advantages of a good Customer Relationship Management (CRM) system is that it provides you with this information, and a lot more. If you currently do not have a robust CRM system in place, then you should add this as one of your strategies for the year ahead.

If you have a clear view of what is in your sales pipeline over the next three to six months and you know what should be coming in and when, and you also have a clear idea of your expenditure over the next six months, then cash flow can be managed quite accurately. As I said, it is not rocket science.

Setting Budgets

Many people find the process of setting budgets frustrating because once they have been set at the start of the year, they're out of date by the end of the month. The reality is that everything is constantly changing around us which is why we need to dynamically measure everything month in, month out and make those small in-flight course corrections

that might be needed. Indeed, not to do so, and to stick to a plan designed for circumstances that have now changed, is a recipe for disaster.

Many of the businesses that I work with are in constant evolution as they quickly adapt to the way the market is slowly changing around them. So, how well are you in tune with your own marketplace?

- Are you a listening business?
- Do you seek feedback?
- Do you act on it?
- How aware are you of the changing expectations and needs of your customers?

If you can keep your finger on the pulse of your business and keep an eye on these changes on a monthly basis, you're able to make decisions quicker, and more confidently.

Earlier, we were looking at capacity in a business and how to measure it. Ensuring that staffing levels keep pace with demand is one of the biggest challenges I find when working with SMEs. Their businesses are very often overtaken with demand, but without the immediate capacity in place to handle it. They need more people in the business but either they don't feel they can afford it, or leave it too late to react.

This is where having absolute clarity on your sales pipeline, on your expenditure, your P&L and hence your cash flow, makes it possible to accurately predict when you can afford a new person and start the recruiting process months before they are needed.

If the figures show that another salesperson is affordable in four months' time, now is when you should be recruiting as it will typically take you as long as four to five months to find the right key person to bring into the business.

The trick to keeping and maintaining growth is recruiting long before you are overtaken by demand, and doing so based on accurate cash flow and on the predictions from your sales pipeline.

On the basis that it will take between three and five months to find the right person, this does build in a buffer so you can be certain that the cash flow predictions you made were accurate. If that is the case, and the business came in as predicted, you can carry on and recruit because now you're ready. The new salesperson will then inject the next level of growth to the business, whatever that might be.

However, if the predicted business didn't materialise and your cash flow is such that now is not the time to expand, then you can delay that recruitment for the next few months. Very often, if you've found the right person, they will need to give a period of notice anyway, so a delay of a starting date of a few months should not be a problem whilst the space for them is found.

Some of the top businesses I work with have a handful of people waiting in the wings to come in and be employed when the cash flows and projects are ready.

The perfect business is when you have good people waiting to join you when you are in a position to bring them in.

And that's good strategy!

Business Growth Indicators from across the business

There are many other Business Growth Indicators to consider, but you need to have a balance across all of the five core strategic objectives and also an understanding of the balance between past, present and future.

You need financial Business Growth Indicators, be that profit - gross or net, revenues, cash flow, and cash reserves.

Sales BGIs

You need sales BGIs. These come from the sales process itself, the sales pipeline, and profitability. Sales are responsible

for profit as well as everything else. How many customers do you have and what revenue do they bring in? Do you monitor this on a regular basis?

One thing that is worth tracking could be the percentage of your most profitable customers versus the rest. This is a very telling Business Growth Indicator.

For example, if you've got your top ten customers producing 80% of your revenue, it might be that in one year's time you want to be reducing that down to 60% or 50%. This would mean that you are not over dependent on a number of big customers.

This is well worth tracking over time. You may want to build in an indicator that alerts you when the business is becoming over reliant on a small number of customers for the bulk of its revenue. Over time, you really want to reduce that reliance and therefore you need to have a strategy underpinning that. How do you do that?

Focusing on continually filling the sales funnel

If you want to reduce reliance on the percentage of top customers, then you need to be focusing on bringing in new customers. Therefore 'New Business' is also another key indicator under sales.

The danger of not monitoring this is that it can mask a bigger problem. Revenues and profitability may be growing over a year and everything might seem fine, but what's actually happening is it's all growing from your current customer base and not from bringing in new customers.

Your current customers are buying more from you, which is fine. However, if that trend continues you just become over reliant on your current customers and not realise that the bigger problem is that you can't bring in new business. It is so easy for this to happen if you are not monitoring the right things.

I was working once with a large technology company that was experiencing this exact problem. They were brilliant at servicing their current customers and they were growing really well. However, all their growth was through their current customers.

They seemed to have an inability to bring in new customers regularly. We started to track new business coming in every month from new sources and put targets in place. We also split out new business in the sales pipeline so it could be measured. This became a Business Growth Indicator.

If you think that this might be an issue for you, you should consider adding that to your Business Growth Indicators.

"What gets measured, gets done."

Marketing BGIs

If your strategy is based around your marketing, then you need to measure your marketing spend in the month. Many people would then measure their spend against their annual marketing budget, but that is only a small part of the bigger picture. What you should be far more interested in is the Return On Investment (ROI) from your marketing spend.

If you are finding it difficult to measure this, then it could be because you haven't got the right marketing systems in place or you might not have the right CRM reporting. One of your strategies might be to put that in place, so that you can measure ROI over a period of time.

You also need to be measuring the results achieved from socio-media, PR activity, email marketing, direct mail, promotions, and also success with exhibitions and events.
Pick the right Business Growth Indicators from your marketing, which provide the best indication of the results you are achieving.

Because marketing can be such a multifaceted part of the business, it might be that it deserves its own separate Strategy on a PageTM sheet. That might also apply to sales where you have different routes to market.

You can split the page into divisions if there are a lot of Business Growth Indicators to be tracked. Alternatively, you might want to drop down a level and use Key Performance Indicators to track all the different aspects of marketing and sales which need to be monitored.

BGIs in Operations

We have already touched on the various forms of measuring operations. They can be about tracking capacity, monitoring quality, customer service or customer satisfaction.

What is important is that you find the right things to measure so that you can instantly see what is happening, or if things are drifting off track. Operations is the heart of the business and can be taken for granted when everything is going well. It is only when you have the right BGIs in place that you can proactively pick up an unhelpful trend long before it becomes a problem.

BGIs in Human Relations / TALENT

Earlier we mentioned that a good BGI is to measure the percentage of PAYE against revenue. You might also want to measure and track recruitment in the business. If it is a fast growing company, you should be recruiting all the time and it might be you would want to have an indicator to measure that. It might also be that you want to find a way of tracking employee satisfaction internally. That might mean measuring values in order to understand how embedded they are across the company as a whole.

Some companies have an unusually high 'churn' with the turnover of staff. Knowing the cost of recruiting and training new staff members is important because if staff are not staying with the company for whatever reason, then you need to understand why. High staff turnover can be a big drain on profits. You might want to look at a way of measuring and monitoring this as part of your BGIs.

Your people are your most important resource and your corporate culture will be the biggest influencing factor affecting why they choose to stay or why they choose to leave.

I have seen companies who absolutely understand this and have evolved a culture in which recognition is the norm, not the exception, and everyone feels valued and appreciated. A very rare achievement within a company and only possible where there is inspired leadership and very clear values that are aligned right across the organisation.

If you look at the layered triangle diagram representing Abraham Maslow's famous Hierarchy of Needs philosophy, you will see how fundamental the need to be appreciated and recognised is in all of us. What symptoms are there that could give you an indication of the corporate culture within your company? How could you measure this? Should it be a BGI?

Maslow's Hierarchy of Needs

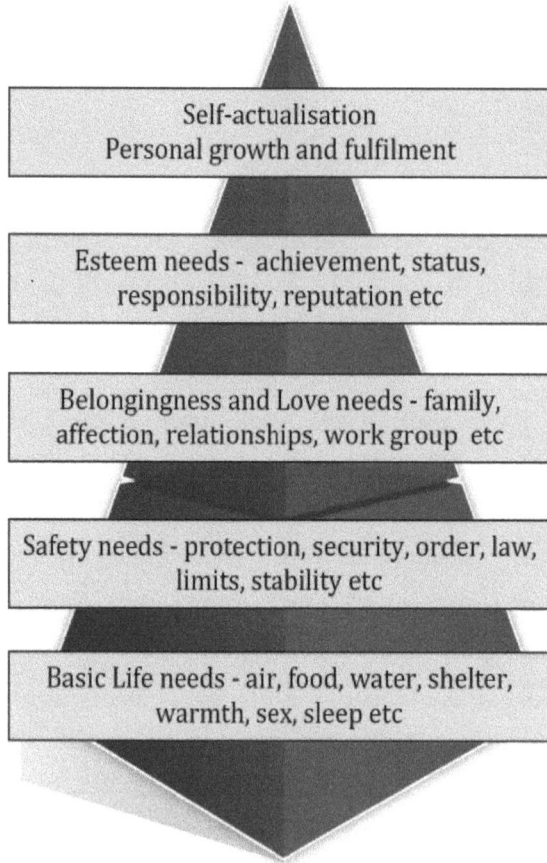

Self-actualisation
Personal growth and fulfilment

Esteem needs - achievement, status,
responsibility, reputation etc

Belongingness and Love needs - family,
affection, relationships, work group etc

Safety needs - protection, security, order, law,
limits, stability etc

Basic Life needs - air, food, water, shelter,
warmth, sex, sleep etc

Self-actualisation Personal growth and fulfilment

Esteem needs - achievement, status, responsibility,
reputation etc

Belongingness and Love needs - family, affection,
relationships, work group etc

Safety needs - protection, security, order, law, limits, stability
etc

Basic Life needs - air, food, water, shelter, warmth, sex,
sleep etc

Bringing your BGI Strategy on a Page™ together

- You now have your purpose of why you exist and. your vision of what it is you're trying to create.

- You have your values of what you stand for, what makes you different, your Unique Selling Proposition

- You know what market space you operate in and, equally important, what space you don't operate in.

- You have clarity on the promise you're making to your customers.

- You also have a clear strategy of how you're going to get there and a long-term strategy, medium term and short-term strategy across all major elements of the business
- Next to that, you now have your Business.

- Growth Indicators and know how you are going to measure your success over time.

- You know the numbers that you are aiming for and what you need to do this month in order to step towards the major objectives and the major strategy of the business.

If you have achieved all of that, congratulations! You are ready to take this on to the next stage.

However, if there are still some aspects of this that you are not sure about, this is the time to stop and backtrack.

Trust me, you will only really benefit from moving on if you have these strong foundations in place.

A role for everyone

It's my belief that everybody in your company should be responsible indirectly or directly for one of the key performance indicators in their role which link into the ultimate Business Growth Indicator and one of the strategies, which is why we cover every area in the page.

If every function is covered on the page, then everybody is aligned to the ultimate purpose and strategy of the business.

If every area of the business is covered in Business Growth Indicators, everybody in the company is ultimately aligned to one of those indicators.

For me, that's where the real power comes in. This is where you get amazing people working in amazing companies, because these days people want to feel aligned and part of something real and significant.

So, I hope that gives you food for thought for your Business Growth Indicators. If you do need a bit more help, there's a lot more resources online, and plenty of videos, so do keep in touch with the Business Growth International website.

But get on to your page now and complete the final sections. In the next chapter, we're going to talk about how you hold yourself accountable and become fully aligned.

"A company that knows who it is and where it is going and is completely in alignment will be a magnet to good people. You won't need to look for them. They will find you."

Key Points

- Your business Growth Indicators align directly to your Key Actions and Timescale. This is where 'the rubber hits the road'

- What numbers should you be doing this month (or sometimes week or quarter)?

- Define the KPIs covering all areas of the business.

- Right! Now, what are your monthly targets?

Success depends upon previous preparation, and without such preparation there is sure to be failure.

Confucius

F.E.A.R

False
Evidence
Appearing
Real

Chapter Nine

Accountability

The F Word

You never thought you'd hear it from me, but I use two F words a lot when I'm speaking to the business leaders. And they may not be what you think!

The two F words I am talking about can completely stop us from taking the action we want to take and can leave us 'caught in the headlights'. Never a safe place to be standing!

The first F word I am talking about is Fear.

I will often ask business leaders what they're scared of in business right now, and what is the one thing they're fearful of happening. And the answers I get are sometimes very telling.

If you were to ask yourself that same question, what would your answer be? Whatever it is for you, then that absolutely needs to be the top one in your five strategic actions.

It could be the fear of firing someone, or getting rid of someone that you need to go.

It might be that for whatever reason, your business partner is holding the business back, and that you need to find a way of exiting from that relationship.

It could be your fear of leaving the company, of separating it, or spinning it off. For some people it could be the fear of making the acquisition or another company. A lot of companies I work with want to do acquisitions but they're scared of it; they're scared of the risk involved. We will look at that scenario later on.

What is it that you fear most in your business? What action are you holding back on taking as a result? Whatever it is, has it been addressed in the strategy you have included on your page already? If not, go back, assess it and tweak the page accordingl

The Second F word is Failure

Another reason for not taking action is the fear of failure. Are you afraid of what might happen if things go wrong? Is this holding you back? Is fear trapping you in a comfort zone? Are you just going for the safe and risk free options and missing opportunities for growth as a result?

In my book 'Life's Great Adventure', I cover the subject of fear in some detail. After all, when you pit yourself again the awesome power of nature by running across an unforgiving desert, or climbing some of the highest mountains in the world, it is not your business that is on the line, but your life itself. A little bit of fear in those circumstances is a very healthy thing and keeps you very focused and alert.

Looking at your current circumstances, and the fear you have for you and your business. Exactly what is it that you are worried that you could fail on?

Let's go back for a moment to the subject of acquisitions. Acquiring another company is a very effective way of growing a business but a lot of companies are scared of them because of the risk that it might fail. Indeed, if you look at the statistics surrounding the success rate of joint ventures and acquisitions, they're pretty poor. However, in my view I believe that the main reason that these go wrong is around the execution and the values piece of the business.

If you get your Strategy on a Page™ right, and you are clear on your values and your strategy moving forward, getting an acquisition right is a lot easier. Looking at your own vision, purpose, values and company promise, and measuring them

against the company you are acquiring will quickly help you to see if it is a true match to your own culture, and to seamlessly become an effective part of your growing organisation. If there is not a match, then you should maybe think twice.

By using your Strategy on a Page™ to guide you through this process, you are taking away much of the uncertainty and the fear of the risk of failure.

Fear of Recruitment

Another area that many companies fear failing with, is that of bringing in new people. Good people are the life blood of a growing business, but the experience of many managers is that they recruit Dr Jekyll at the interview, but it is Mr Hyde who arrives to take up the job. Getting it wrong can be a costly mistake. Every company will have stories on getting the recruitment process spectacularly wrong.

Is that fear holding you back from growing? Are you afraid of getting it wrong and damaging the business as a result? Earlier in the book, we spoke about the power of your Vision, Purpose and Values and also your Company Promise. When you get them right, not only does it have a powerful effect on the way your business is perceived by your customers, but also how it is seen by prospective employees who are drawn towards what you stand for as a business. You become a magnet for good people.

When that happens, you are no long in the business of kissing frogs in the hope of finding a prince, and fear surrounding the recruitment process will vanish.

So I ask you again,
what's your fear of failure?
What could you fail on?

What are you scared of in business right now?
Now, go and readdress your strategy and ensure that those things are being dealt with.

The Fear of Regret

When I am working with a business leader, I like to invite them to look five years' forward. I'll say to them, "Forget about the fears you have right now and the worries you have about the risk of failing. What if you sat here in five years' time and you're doing exactly the same thing as you are doing now, but instead of growing, you've gone backwards. What if you're in the same position doing the same job in the same place. What does that look like?"

This is never a pleasant thought to contemplate and the looks I see on the leaders' faces are humbling, to say the least. Imagine getting to the end of this work life, in whatever guise that may be, looking back and just wishing you'd done a number of things that you haven't done, and think of the pain of that regret.

The worst thing about it would be that the reason you haven't done them is because the fear of failure that you have right now.

So, take a look again at your business, ensure all the strategies are in place, that you're addressing your fears head on and that that fear and risk of failure is addressed in the strategy and being mitigated.

So, who holds you accountable?

Accountability is the big question and it has been the biggest driver for me in creating the Strategy on a Page™ software for those who can't afford true accountability through coaches or consultants. Everybody needs a mentor, everyone needs to be held accountable in business in one way or another, even Bill Gates has a mentor. His mentor is Warren Buffett.

Now, within BGI, we're creating a network of mentors. I personally mentor numerous companies in the UK and all over the world, and we take that position of accountability.

For you to achieve your full potential, you need to have somebody you can hold yourself accountable to. Without that, we will get away with making excuses to ourselves, and believing them!

You could use a BGI mentor, but it could be anybody. It could be a business coach, it could be your business partner, but I think it works best when you use a professional and not somebody close to you.

If you start getting your wife/husband to hold you accountable or a close friend, there's a lack of objectivity because they are emotionally involved.

They are not detached from the business and will not be able to see it from a neutral standpoint. Whatever you do, you need to hold yourself accountable to somebody external to the company. In my experience, it is very rare that an individual can effectively hold themselves to account and achieve their full potential.

I practice what I preach here. I have several mentors; Tony Wilson from Lifestyle Architecture is my mentor and holds me accountable to my strategy on one of my companies. I have a mentor in speaking; Roger Harrop, who holds me accountable to my speaking strategy.and continue to seek out experts to help me in the emerging fields in business like AI.

What does true accountability mean?

Well, in terms of the page, if you use it in the way it has been designed, it will indeed provide a powerful way to keep you accountable.

For a start, there are the five strategic actions which you have identified to do this month. Then there's the six, or seveneight, business growth indicators that you have identified that you will use to measure your progress at the end of the month. On the BGI Strategy on a Page™ Application software we have made, this is really easy to do.

But the question is, did you do it? We are all human and we can easily give ourselves a very plausible reason for not doing the things which we know that we should be doing, but are uncomfortable. Very often, this will be because we know we have not achieved what we have put on the page in one or two areas. Instead of facing this, it is far easier to find an excuse to put it to one side. These are usually the things that affect the areas where we're fearful or there's a risk of failure. There is no escape from the fact that the page holds you accountable to all of them at all times.

How does accountability work? I find a very powerful way of tracking where I am on multiple projects or tasks is to use a simple colour coding system. I use the BGI Strategy on a Page™ app to colour code (but you could easily use a set of coloured highlighter pens) to alert me at a glance to what needs to be done right now. I will print off a copy of my Key Actions at the start of each month, and highlight each one as follows:

Any task that that you have completed, highlight in Green. If you didn't do it, it's Red. So far, so good – and not rocket science.

Now, there's two other colours, which we use very sparingly. One is an Amber. That means you did everything you could to achieve this task, but it's ever so slightly not done because of somebody else's fault.

We need, first of all, for there to be accountability, for there to be somebody who is responsible for enforcing standards and holding people's feet to the fire.

Jennifer Granholm

Let me give you an example of an Amber. You said you were going to sign legal contracts with a JV or a solicitor. You've done everything you could and now you're just waiting on a solicitor. So an Amber is where you've done everything you said you were going to do, but you're waiting on somebody else to take the action.

The other colour is Grey. I use this sparingly in a situation where a task that has been hanging about for some time waiting to be completed has been overtaken and is no longer relevant. It can be taken off the page.

It might be that you've delegated it out to another member of staff because you've realised it's not something you should be doing. It could be it shouldn't have been on the page in the first place; believe me, this happens.

Now, as you start to working on Strategy on a Page™, there should be very few Greys over the first few months. However, as you start moving into the six month period, you may start to realise that there are some tasks that are no longer important and that's where the Grey would be used.

Using colour to bring your page alive

The brain was never designed to work in black and white; it loves colour. That is why colourful Mind Maps are so brain friendly. Therefore use colour to bring your page alive and to give it another dimension.

Spotting trends

You can use the same colour coding for your business growth indicators. For example, you will have all the numbers on the page that you had planned to achieve. Now you need to add in the numbers that actually happened.

If you said you were going to do twenty thousand in revenues and you do twenty one thousand in revenues, then you highlight that number with a Green. However, If you only did nineteen thousand five hundred, very close, you get an Amber. But if you are way off, by which I mean more than 5-10% off, then it's a Red because you didn't do what you said you were going to do.

Use this same system for all your key actions and all business growth indicators every month and you will find it really makes the page a far more powerful tool.

The other advantage of using the 'traffic light' colour coding system is that you can use it to get a quick helicopter view of the trends in your business by looking back over your pages for the past few months.

Now, this exercise is very quick. You are not drilling down into detail, but simply looking at one subject, or task, and tracking the colour of it over the past few months. If it is green all the way, you are doing well. If you have a larger than average number of reds, then that should be telling you something. What you get is a trend.

You can get a trend every single month for each of the five core strategic actions. Obviously, these are major to the business and it gives you the chance to compare what you commit to doing every month with what you actually did.

You should do the same thing with your business growth indicators, which is a powerful way to hold you to account. By doing this, it allows you to take strategic actions very quickly and months before any other business would typically make a decision. It is such a simple tool to use, and yet what it tells you is priceless. It also very quickly highlights those areas where you're weak and where you're kidding yourself. We are all really good at that!

Using this simple system, what you quickly find, from the flashes of red, is that you may be giving yourself more to do than is realistically possible. Alternatively, you may find that you are committing yourself to do what is achievable, but it is not being prioritised over penny tasks, or that other things are being allowed to get in the way. Either way, it is an indication that you need to step up and take the action you needed to take.

When you get this accountability every month on your core strategic actions, it is holding a mirror up to yourself.

You'll easily be able to spot where your strengths are, which is reassuring, but also those area you're kidding yourself in business and need to take action.

'Management by Looking like a Twit'

One of my clients, who's very bright, Oxford educated and who's into the leadership and management theories, asked me what school of leadership theory Strategy on a Page™ came out of. He was interested if it was influenced by an MBA programme or if it was some leadership theorem.

For me, I have always thought it was just plain common sense and I had not given it a label. But he pressed me to give it a name. So I flippantly said, "It's called 'Management by Looking like a Tw*t'."

When he dug deeper I explained: "If you're very clear on the purpose of your company and you have mapped your strategy and you know what you should be doing every month; if you have five core strategic actions every month to step you towards your ultimate vision and purpose of your strategy; and every month if you hold yourself accountable to somebody else and you keep coming to the table and you haven't done what you said you were going to do, you are going to look like a twit."

"What is more, if you come back the next month again, and you still haven't done what you were going to do, and that continues for several months, you're going to look like a bigger twit, until you have so much pain associated with not doing it because you're looking so stupid in front of other people, that you end up doing the action you should have done in the first place." So, Management by Looking like a Twit.

If you are holding yourself accountable to the five core strategic actions that need to be done in the month, you are very much in control of your business. If there is some action that has not been taken, it's going to have a knock-on effect on the business growth indicators and you will see this right away. Cause and Effect.

Case Study

One company I've been working with is a telecoms company called Direct Response. It is a fantastic company and has been growing for many years. Chris Robinson, the CEO, is amazing along with Ian Mitchell, the MD, who's running that whole telecoms division, and Adam Tilson, MD of the Call Centre arm. They are all excellent strategically.

However, there was one area that they had identified that they were weak at. This was in the area of recruiting additional sales people. For a variety of reasons, this was something that they had been putting off and really not getting round to doing. And that became evident on the page.

Using the colour coding 'traffic light' system, they quickly noticed that they had several reds and ambers, and as a result, they got on with it and recruited the various sales people they needed.

There is no coincidence that directly four to six months following that action being taken, the revenues increased significantly because the sales people were then coming through and delivering.

If they had continually ignored those reds and ambers and if they hadn't been on the page, it would have been very easy to overlook this issue completely, which would have had a significant impact on their bottom line. Having the BGIs in place, it was identified quickly, they took action and the problem was fixed.

If you are putting off hiring that sales person, it will be directly affecting what your revenues will be in the future and this will affect your core strategy in that area.

Using this system, you will be able to see significant trends over time and the result of actions being taken or not being taken. Action and Reaction. As Scottie says in Star Trek, "Ye cannae change the laws of physics!"

Quicker decision making

Let's have a look at the business growth indicators. Again, the power of accountability here enables us to make decisions in business far quicker than we would normally be able to. For example, if you're trending by using your colour marker system, you will be following revenues, profitability, pipeline, and the percentage of new business. So, here's what happens.

If your percentage of new business is flashing red, identifying that you need to be bringing in an amount of new business that month, and if this continues to flash red in the following months as well, then you will see other indicators start to flash as well.

Next, you will see that your pipeline of future business also starts flashing red. If you ignore this as well, I can guarantee you one thing: in about three to four months following that, your revenues will flash red as a direct consequence.

The system help you to pick up these trends really quickly and to act very fast as a result, long before a trend becomes a real problem.

"An expert is someone who has succeeded in making decisions and judgements simpler through knowing what to pay attention to and what to ignore."

Edward de Bono

The Myth of a Bad Month

In my book, there is never such a thing as a 'Bad Month' because this implies that having a good month or a bad month is something that you have no control over.

I have companies coming to me for the first time complaining that they are having a bad month. The reality is that they are not having a bad month now, but they had a bad month four months ago and didn't realise it because they weren't measuring it at the time. If they had been measuring it, and trending, they would have taken action then and solved the problem well in advance of it happening.

By putting the right business growth indicators in place, it allows us to recognise when we're going to have a bad month coming up and, more importantly, put in the right strategic action to mitigate against it.

If you start to see that your pipeline is flashing red based on what revenues you want to project, and you see that your new business is also flashing red, you

need to have a significant sales drive underpinning that as a strategic action for the following month. If you don't do something differently, if you carry on business as usual, it will affect your top-line at some point, and your bottom line. It's just a matter of time.

A bad month doesn't happen without warning. If you are measuring the right things, you can spot a bad month coming towards you well in advance. That is the real benefit of Strategy on a Page™.

You can stay in control of your business by holding yourself accountable on a month-by-month basis for both the strategic actions and also with your business growth indicators.

In addition, by tracking historic trends it is possible to proactively take decisions months before they would normally be taken. You can be far more responsive and impact the growth of the business faster, quicker and more effectively.

Case Study

To give you another example of this, a media company I was doing some work with recently had exactly this issue. We came in and discovered that they'd never really measured pipeline before. They'd had a pretty good performance last year and the growth was strong, their revenues were strong and so was their profitability. That was really all they were measuring; revenue and profitability. But was this giving them the full picture?

We then put the following indicators in place. We put in pipeline, and a BGI surrounding the percentage of that, which was new business from new clients.

This quickly highlighted that the fact that their business came from around about twenty different customers but they were very over reliant on three of them, which made up a disproportionately large percentage of their turnover.

Up until that point, they'd never really measured pipeline before and just accepted the business that seemed to be just magically appearing on a month-by-month basis. Neither were they really measuring cash flows.

Now, at this point they wanted to grow, and to do so they needed to recruit quite a lot of people. So, for them, cash flow was key. Obviously, you can't just go recruiting people willy-nilly without knowing if you can afford to pay them or not. We needed to help them to understand pipeline and also the expenditure model to make sure that it would be possible to cash flow the growth moving forward. We also needed to put cash reserves in place to ensure this could happen.

When we did all that, what became evident was that their pipeline for new business was at red, in fact it was virtually at zero. In addition, their pipeline for the next three months was also a red, but they didn't believe that this could possibly be the case.

As it so happens, it was the case, which provided the point that if you rely on emotions and feeling rather than facts, you can get into deep water very quickly

Chapter Ten

Alignment

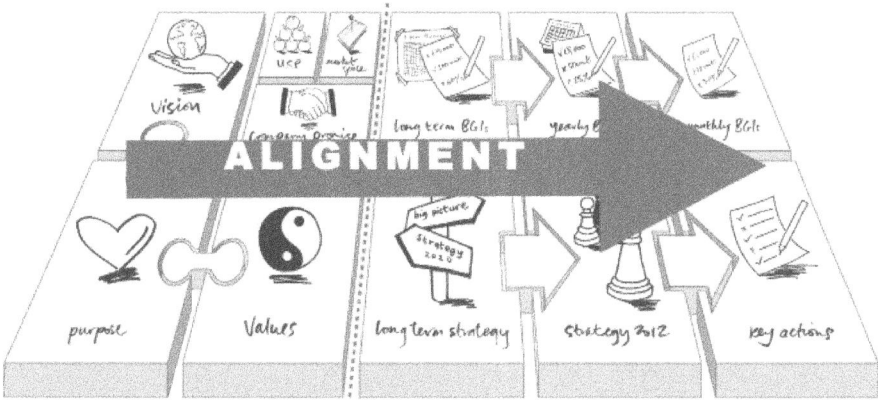

I know, you don't have to say it, but this book has echoes of 'Catch 22'. Every time you think that you've cracked it and you have completed your Strategy on a Page™, up pops another chapter, with "and here's another thing!" But you know that I would never short change you, so let's talk about Alignment.

Now you've got your strategy on the page. You have your purpose, your vision, your values. You have blocked out your long-term, medium-term and short- term strategies, and put in place your business growth indicators to measure them. You have even chosen the best way for you to hold yourself to account on a month-by-month basis. Finally, you have adopted the principle of trending and invested in a sparkling new set of colour highlighter pens. It's just like going back to school after the holidays.

Now at this stage, it is you and only you who have achieved clarity on all of this stuff. If it were to stop there, and you just kept it to yourself, you would be missing a big trick.

The next thing to do is to share this throughout the company and get true alignment. Of course, it starts with you as a leader, but ultimately you need to get this through your whole company. They need to know where they sit in this big picture and their role in creating a future that they can be proud of. There is only one way to make dramatic change within a company, and that is from the top down. It can never happen from the bottom up, but surprisingly that is the way many businesses start. Corporate culture emanates from the leader. They always take their cue, from you.

Before we move into the alignment of your staff, let's talk about the alignment with you. The page, which we have painstakingly put together over the last ten chapters is unique to you as the CEO, MD or leader in your organisation. It's the essence of who you are. We've gone into the depths of purpose and ultimately that purpose is yours.

Public and private versions of the page

Now, I understand that some of that stuff you wouldn't want to share with everybody. It may be commercially sensitive for one thing. So, very often in an organisation, we have two separate pages; one for the leader and another page for all the employees, and they're subtly different.

For example, in a small business many of the strategies are quite personal to the business owner and may relate to money goals and lifestyle required for the leaders.

Clearly, that is not a wise thing to be sharing with the rest of the employees.

The other thing that you might not want to become public is if you have plans to exit the company. Going for a sale can be very good business practice and could be good for the employees. As a result of it, a number of senior staff would be groomed into more senior positions. Nevertheless, for them to learn about this too far in advance, and without the bigger picture being shared with them, it could have an unsettling effect on the business.

Therefore, understand that you need to have your own page which you will be using to steer the business forward, hold yourself accountable, and stay on track. In addition, you will have a further page to share with your employees, and other stakeholders. This version will retain the same values, your USP, your market space and your promise, which doesn't change, ever. It is that which you want to get buy-in right across the company. What you might word differently, however, are those detailed elements of strategy which are either commercially sensitive, or inappropriate for a more general audience.

You have your page as the leader, which you need to be completely aligned to, which by default, you should be. You've created the page, so your alignment should be total. But that on its own is not enough. You also need to ensure that your systems, your productivity, your day-to-day tools, are also aligned to the page as well, to ensure that it's being actioned appropriately.

For example, if you use a life planner, a time management system, or a to-do list, this needs to play a part in supporting you by keeping your key actions and BGIs visible to you on a daily basis .

Whatever you're using to encourage your actions, whether online or offline, just make sure that that is aligned to the page so the action is filtered down to whatever it should be. This is essential. The contents of your page needs to be a part of your daily decision- making process and a way of helping to focus of the aspects of it that have the greatest priority for the business.

Without this, your page will just sit there and be ineffective. You might have your five core activities but they won't filter down to the day-to-day activity of actions within the company.

You may have other systems, like a Customer Relationship Management system, email marketing engine, or lead capture processes. Everything has to be aligned to the page in some way.

Getting everyone on board

The next stage of the process is to ensure that every individual within the company is aligned to the page. Now, this is where it gets very interesting!

When you introduce the public version of your page to the company, it's a really good time to assess whether everybody's on the bus or not.

I was working once with a £2½ million pound company operating with 22 staff. Having successfully helped them to create their page and to get clarity on the direction they were moving in, we looked at the team they had in place to make this happen and see if they were in alignment to this.

It became clear that one person wasn't aligned to the page, which in small companies is not unusual. It is so important to identify this early in the process. Having done so, it may just mean that the individual in question just needs a bit of encouragement or a little bit of training to get them in alignment. In other cases, they may have evolved into a bit of an internal terrorist.

This could seriously jeopardise your plans for moving forward.

If by introducing the pag,e you discover that there is somebody in your company who is not just out of alignment, but is in danger or undermining your efforts, then obviously this cannot be allowed to continue.

You can't afford to have anyone on board who you don't trust, or is working against you. So, whilst you are introducing the page, keep your wits about you, keep very aware of what's going on with all the employees.

Introducing the Page to your team

There's lots of different ways to introduce the page; it depends on how big your company is. It could be that the right time is at the annual company meetings. Alternatively, you might want to introduce it to individual teams through smaller meetings or workshops

If it's just you and your dog, then you could just tell your dog about it. That might sound flippant, but actually it's not. The more opportunities you have to talk about this stuff and put it into words, the better. Every time you do it, you will get greater clarity yourself. So, do tell your dog!

"The factories of the future will have only two employees, a man and a dog. The man is there to feed the dog. The dog is there to keep the man from touching the equipment."

Earlier in the book, I referred to Maslow's 'Hierarchy of Needs'. If you are not familiar with his work, then go look him up on Wikipedia. His research helped him to form the conclusion that everybody needs to have an activity that gives them a sense of contribution, in order to feel self-valued and to be recognised.

There is no better way to do this than to share the 'big picture' of your purpose, vision and values for the business that they are a part of. By inspiring them with your plans to grow the organisation, and what it could mean for them, is hugely empowering. Instead of just 'doing a job', they can see themselves in a far bigger context, with huge benefit to them as the company goals are progressively achieved and new opportunities emerge as a result. Now, this should be incredibly exciting to everyone in the company.

It may have been the case in the past that people just clocked in, did a day's work and clocked out with no real engagement or even interest in the company as a whole, but we have come a long way from the days of the 'dark satanic mills'.

Today things are very different. People want to feel part of something bigger, they want to feel aligned to some purpose, they want to feel like they're useful. Sharing the page with them for the first time can therefore be very powerful.

How to share 'the Page'

When you share the page, it does need to cascade from the top downwards. There are wonderful examples, particularly in the world of retail when it was thought that by just changing the attitude and behaviour of the staff at the sharp end of the business, a business could be turned round, without the directors or managers being involved at all. It never worked! You can't have two cultures running side by side in any organisation.

Either everybody is on the page, or they are not. It can only start at the top at director level, then down to senior management, and down to departmental heads, and so forth.

This gives you the opportunity to make it personal and relevant to them, and for them to ask questions that relate to their areas of responsibility.

When you introduce the page, do so from the left hand side to the right.

Start by talking about what you stand for, and the very purpose of the business. Share with them the ultimate vision of who you are as a business or organisation and what it is that you are trying to create.

Then move on to the values, the expectations we have of each other and how we express that in the way we behave. What is acceptable, and what is not, and how we should support each other in the process.

Share the unique selling proposition of the business and how that makes you different. Talk about the market space you operate in and the promise we're going to deliver to our customers. Don't rush this. It is too important.

Having explained the way you see the business and how you want it to be seen in the marketplace, then move on to your strategy of how you will get there.

Explain the long-term strategy and the key components for each of the departments, the medium-term strategy in the year, and then the short-term actions. This is what you need to do this month and who's responsible for those key actions.

Explain also the Business Growth Indicators and describe the way that they will be measured on a monthly basis.

Now, all of this is really powerful stuff, but equally powerful is the fact that you are sharing it with them. You are showing them great respect by letting them 'inside' the company. They are not just 'workers', but trusted and appreciated colleagues. You are demonstrating that this is not a 'them and us' business, but that you are all in it together. This is not just empty words or corporate spin, but something very real that they can see, touch. You are giving them the opportunity to engage with and be a meaningful part of the business moving forward. Very empowering.

As a result of all this, they should fully understand, probably for the first time, not just what it is their company is all about and what it delivers, but also what it stands for.

They will also understand how their contribution plays a vital role in helping the company achieve its goals, and what that means to them in terms of their future, their security and their own future prospects. It gives them a great reason to want to be 'on the bus' rather than waiting for it to arrive!

An important part of this process is to encourage feedback and input. The best time for this is at the event where you are sharing all of this stuff. Doing this in public makes sure that everyone understands and has the chance to ask questions and challenge you to share your passion and vision. Take time to make sure they all 'get it'; some might take a little longer than others

There is always one!

Inevitably, the law of averages states that not everyone will share your vision. There will always be someone who sits at the back of the room and who is plainly not only on a different page, but in a different book altogether! Sharing your vision with the team and getting them all on your page is vital for your business. You cannot afford to have two separate factions running within your company pulling against each other. At the end of the day, it is your bat and your ball, and you decide who comes out to play.

I know how dangerous a negative influence can be in an organisation. It only takes one cynic who knows the price of everything, but the value of nothing, to undermine your efforts and be a rallying point for discontent. Dealing with that is never easy, but deal with it you must.

It may be that you have inherited some staff from a previous merger or past incarnation of the company and it wasn't possible to deal with this before now, but if you have a disruptive or negative person on board, simply containing them and countering the effect they are having on everyone else is going to sap energy.

If you have yet to address this issue, then you need to toughen up and face it. It absolutely needs to be one of the actions on your page. You can only achieve your big goals with the right people around you and no hostages!

As a leader, we need to lead through good times, and bad. I don't like getting rid of people but I've had to fire my fair share over the years. It never gets easier, but I always know that I'm doing it for the right reasons

At the end of the day, if somebody is not happy and makes no secret of the fact, then it is in their interests as much as yours to help them find an opportunity that is better suited to their needs.

Also from the company's point of views, an internal terrorist can bring the entire energy of the whole company down, not just the individual leader themselves.

So, by getting rid of a bad apple in the company, you can actually positively affect the morale of the entire company by doing so and create a legend by doing so, but more on this in a later chapter.

Alignment in Action

In launching the Page to every layer of management and all the employees in that business, never forget the power of sharing aspects of it with other stakeholders, partners, associates, investors, and even customers. Any organisation who is really clear of who they are, what they stand for, what their core objectives are and who they serve, will be admired and respected. It can be hugely reassuring to customers to deal with a business that they too can feel aligned to.

As far as internally within the company is concerned, the first stage is to get everybody aligned to the vision and purpose, and for them to have clarity in their role of delivering it.

The next stage is to use the page as part of your recruitment process. You can start to test this at CV stage or application stage. If you look at most of the major corporations, when they're asking applications to be filled in, most of these are values based in parts.

"We must all wage an intense, lifelong battle against the constant downward pull. If we relax, the bugs and weeds of negativity will move into the garden and take away everything of value."

Jim Rohn

If they get through that, then you would continue in the same way at a face-to-face interview where you would weave in values based questions into your interview techniques. You might also use psychometric evaluation tools, as these have proved to be very effective. You cannot afford to hire the wrong person.

When you get to the final stages of interviews, you can share more of the left hand side of the page with them to help them to buy into the philosophy of the company and see for themselves whether they are a match or not.

Once you've finally got the person that you think you want to recruit in front of you, that's the point when you bring out the rest of the page. This is not something you would do earlier as it is quite a confidential document. However, if by now you potentially have your new operations manager sitting in front of you, it is a great opportunity to share your vision and the big picture that they would be a part of delivering.

You might say, "We think you'll be a fit with us, and also that we will be a fit with you. I now want to share with you what the grand plan for this company is and our core strategy." At that point, you would bring out the full page and share it with them in the same way that you did with your current team. If they are not excited, wowed and just waiting to bite your hand off to start working at the company, you've probably about to recruit the wrong person. So, watch their reactions very carefully.

It's a fantastic final test to just see how people are aligned and if they are bought into the purpose and vision. Because if they're not bought into it at that point of interview, I guarantee they won't be bought into it when they start in your company.

Be warned. It's just like getting married. You only have one chance to get this right!

"The most important question to ask about a job is not, 'What will I earn?' but 'What will I become?' as a result of joining the organisation."

Jim Rohn

Appraisals on the Page

Not only do we use the page to align our current employees and as a tool to recruit new members of the team, but we can also use it as an ongoing appraisal tool. In the same way that you are measuring your BGIs against your core strategies, so also during the day-to-day process of managing the business, you can measure people's performance against the page.

With the page in place, staff appraisals are not just the once a year process that many businesses put their people through without really understanding what it is they are doing it for, but it can be a continuous process when you have the page to refer to and measure against.

By the way, if you do appraisals at yearly intervals, you are leaving it far too long and probably using them for the wrong reasons anyway.

However, by using the page as the basis of measurement, it is very different because you have clear objectives:

- Give feedback to employees on their performance
- Quickly identify their training needs
- Learn from the individual about their experiences with processes or operations, and use that information to make improvements to the business as a whole
- Improve communication
- Share issues or problems
- Demonstrate the context of the employee's role to the business as a whole

Use the results to inform personnel decisions, such as salary increases, promotions, or the need to instigate a disciplinary process. Share short and medium terms strategy and objectives

Reinforce vision and values

Because using the page in this way is so powerful, and the results so easy to quantify, many people are now doing this with their employees every three or four months. This help them stay totally aligned, and also it provides you with the information necessary to make those small course corrections early and before issues arise.

Alignment throughout the company

Now you have everybody at all levels aligned within the company. You've parted company with those people who were not aligned, and who chose to not change and you have also made sure that anybody new coming into the company is aligned properly through the way that you now recruit. We can now move on to cascading this out even further.

Now, depending on the size of the company, there are different ways of doing this.

For a smaller company, one page for the business is more than enough, and individuals have obviously their own systems for action on a day-to-day, week-to-week basis. In larger companies, you may need multiple pages, which would filter down through the organisation.

Individual Pages

What you have now is the ultimate page, which holds the company accountable. You have the divisional pages below it, each being owned by the divisional owners or the divisional unit heads, and now you have the individuals in that company each holding the home page.

When you get down to a page for an individual manager or staff member, it's important that an element of purpose and an element of vision is their own, their personal vision. It might be that they want to be promoted, it may be they want to develop professionally, or grow their skill base.

It may be they want to change offices or go abroad with the company.

Now, we're getting them aligned, not only to the company vision and the company purpose, but the divisional purpose and divisional vision, and now their own. This is where the magic truly happens when this goes right down to an individual level, because you then have an individual who has their own five core strategic priorities, and their own key actions to follow.

For them, it's their own personal strategy, rather than company strategy, and what they need to be doing this month and how they're going to be measured against that. Just think of the power if everyone in the company was working in that way!

Now, what they're doing in the month aligns directly to the divisional strategy, which aligns to the company strategy. The KPIs they're being measured on align directly to the divisional KPIs, which themselves align directly to the company BGIs.

Now you have true alignment as you are all, literally, singing from the same hymn sheet.

Each individual recognises that the actions that they're doing in this month really mean something. It actually impacts the division and the company. They see with total clarity how alignments happen in their company, that they are important, that they are a very important part of the whole process.

They can see how their daily and weekly actions contribute to the divisional activity and the group activity. They can now feel truly aligned and part of something important. If you thought that the original business page was exciting, when you get it down to the individual level, it just gets even more powerful.

It really is incredible the power you now have in your hands as a business owner, leader or manager. In addition, you also have the additional accountability tool now with the Strategy on a Page™ softwareapplication to use in conjunction with your page.

Alternatively, you may have chosen to use your personal business mentor to hold you accountable to the actions on your page.

Now, you've aligned yourself, your main managers or senior management and your staff to that page, so you've got flow throughout the company. You will quickly see that the magic is already starting to work.

However, before you relax or get complacent, yes, there is something else. There always is!

We will now take it deeper and bring your strategy alive in three ways. We do it through putting rhythm and pulse through the company, creating legend and putting in and instilling a really exciting theme

"Success is nothing more than a few simple disciplines, practised every day; while failure issimply a few errors in judgement, repeated every day.

It is the accumulative weight of our disciplines and our judgements that leads us to either fortune or failure."

Jim Rohn

Case Study

I once worked with a large telecoms company who have created a separate page for each of their divisions. They have one overall page for their telecoms business, but because it is part of a wider group, there was a group page above that.

Below the main page for the telecoms business, there's several other pages. The sales division has its own page, and so does the marketing division and also operations.

The point is that the main page we have been creating is that it is what holds the whole company accountable, including the diversity in all the different divisions. The page is a blend of operations, sales, marketing, HR and finance. But if you need to go down to the next level, there's no stopping you actually having a page specifically for each of the divisions, as was the case with the telecoms company.

Now, the beautiful thing about creating divisional pages is that most of the work is already done for you.

The left hand side of the page hardly changes. Your purpose, vision, values, USP, market space and promise all remain the same.

It is possible, however, that you might want to describe the purpose of that division, as it is a macro business in its own right. This could also slightly change your description of your vision as well, to give it a departmental focus.

If you're doing a strategy for a financial unit of the business, then the focus would be different again. For example, the branding piece would not be so relevant. However, you might want to describe a very specific vision for that department whilst that aligns it with the rest of the company.

On your main page for the company as a whole, you then break down into the subcomponents of strategy, to make it totally divisionally related.

So, within marketing there will be all the various themes of marketing spreading through the page. For your strategies and key actions, you may have a PR element, online element, offline element, branding development, advertising and social media.

By the time you get to the pages for the divisions, rather than referring to the headings as Business Growth Indicators, you'll probably call them Key Performance Indicators. They are not about the business as a whole, but rather the activities of that division.

Earlier on we were speaking about Return on Investment in relation to your marketing. This is the place where you would monitor those figures and also plot the trends using the 'traffic light' system we covered earlier.

You may be measuring trends in social media, online traffic and visitor statistics, pay-per-click traffic and conversions, whatever it may be. This simple system helps you to keep track of it and to instantly see trends starting to happen. With the one piece of paper, you are in complete control of your division

Back to the telecoms company I was referring to earlier. They have a main company to manage the group, a separate telecoms arm, a call centre's arm and a new technology arm. When I first started working with them, they were all operating under one banner, but it became apparent that the strategies for each part of the business were incredibly different. It was not practical to try and squeeze everything onto one page so we created the individual pages for each division Now these guys have taken it even further.

In the telecoms company, every individual manager has their own page. This has proved to be a massively powerful way of using the page within their business.

Key Points

- Have your own Page as a leader, as big change always happens from the top down in a company

- All systems need to be aligned to the page, like CRM, P&L, operational efficiency etc.

- Introduce the Page to all of your team through annual meet- ings, workshops or smaller man- agement meetings

- Keep a look out for those who are not on board… there's nor-- mally one!

- Use the page to run staff appraisals

- Each department of the company can have individual pages under the main umbrella one

---

Chapter Eleven

Creating Legend

I know, you don't have to say it, but this book has echoes of 'Catch 22'. Every time you think that you've cracked it and you have completed your **Strategy on a Page**™, up pops another chapter, with "and here's another thing!" But you know that I would never short change you, so let's talk about Alignment.

Now you've got your strategy on the page. You have your purpose, your vision, your values. You have blocked out your long-term, medium-term and short- term strategies, and put in place your business growth indicators to measure them. You have even chosen the best way for you to hold yourself to account on a month-by-month basis. Finally, you have adopted the principle of trending and invested in a sparkling new set of colour highlighter pens. It's just like going back to school after the holidays.

Now at this stage, it is you and only you who have achieved clarity on all of this stuff. If it were to stop there, and you just kept it to yourself, you would be missing a big trick.
The next thing to do is to share this throughout the company and get true alignment. Of course, it starts with you as a leader, but ultimately you need to get this through your whole company. They need to know where they sit in this big picture and their role in creating a future that they can be proud of.

There is only one way to make dramatic change within a company, and that is from the top down. It can never happen from the bottom up, but surprisingly that is the way many businesses start. Corporate culture emanates from the leader. They always take their cue, from you.

Before we move into the alignment of your staff, let's talk about the alignment with you. The page, which we have painstakingly put together over the last ten chapters is unique to you as the CEO, MD or leader in your organisation. It's the essence of who you are. We've gone into the depths of purpose and ultimately that purpose is yours.

Public and private versions of the page

Now, I understand that some of that stuff you wouldn't want to share with everybody. It may be commercially sensitive for one thing. So, very often in an organisation, we have two separate pages; one for the leader and another page for all the employees, and they're subtly different.

For example, in a small business many of the strategies are quite personal to the business owner and may relate to money goals and lifestyle required for the leaders. Clearly, that is not a wise thing to be sharing with the rest of the employees.

The other thing that you might not want to become public is if you have plans to exit the company. Going for a sale can be very good business practice and could be good for the employees. As a result of it, a number of senior staff would be groomed into more senior positions. Nevertheless, for them to learn about this too far in advance, and without the bigger picture being shared with them, it could have an unsettling effect on the business.

Therefore, understand that you need to have your own page which you will be using to steer the business forward, hold yourself accountable, and stay on track. In addition, you will have a further page to share with your employees, and other stakeholders. This version will retain the same values, your USP, your market space and your promise, which doesn't change, ever. It is that which you want to get buy-in right across the company. What you might word differently, however, are those detailed elements of strategy which are either commercially sensitive, or inappropriate for a more general audience.

You have your page as the leader, which you need to be completely aligned to, which by default, you should be. You've created the page, so your alignment should be total. But that on its own is not enough. You also need to ensure that your systems, your productivity, your day-to-day tools, are also aligned to the page as well, to ensure that it's being actioned appropriately.

For example, if you use a life planner, a time management system, or a to-do list, this needs to play a part in supporting you by keeping your key actions and BGIs visible to you on a daily basis .

Whatever you're using to encourage your actions, whether online or offline, just make sure that that is aligned to the page so the action is filtered down to whatever it should be. This is essential. The contents of your page needs to be a part of your daily decision- making process and a way of helping to focus of the aspects of it that have the greatest priority for the business.

Without this, your page will just sit there and be ineffective. You might have your five core activities but they won't filter down to the day-to-day activity of actions within the company.

You may have other systems, like a Customer Relationship Management system, email marketing engine, or lead capture processes. Everything has to be aligned to the page in some way.

Getting everyone on board

The next stage of the process is to ensure that every individual within the company is aligned to the page. Now, this is where it gets very interesting! When you introduce the public version of your page to the company, it's a really good time to assess whether everybody's on the bus or not.

I was working once with a £2½ million pound company operating with 22 staff. Having successfully helped them to create their page and to get clarity on the direction they were moving in, we looked at the team they had in place to make this happen and see if they were in alignment to this.

It became clear that one person wasn't aligned to the page, which in small companies is not unusual. It is so important to identify this early in the process. Having done so, it may just mean that the individual in question just needs a bit of encouragement or a little bit of training to get them in alignment. In other cases, they may have evolved into a bit of an internal terrorist.

This could seriously jeopardise your plans for moving forward.

If by introducing the page you discover that there is somebody in your company who is not just out of alignment, but is in danger or undermining your efforts, then obviously this cannot be allowed to continue.

You can't afford to have anyone on board who you don't trust, or is working against you. So, whilst you are introducing the page, keep your wits about you, keep very aware of what's going on with all the employees.

Introducing the Page to your team

There's lots of different ways to introduce the page; it depends on how big your company is. It could be that the right time is at the annual company meetings. Alternatively, you might want to introduce it to individual teams through smaller meetings or workshops

If it's just you and your dog, then you could just tell your dog about it. That might sound flippant, but actually it's not. The more opportunities you have to talk about this stuff and put it into words, the better. Every time you do it, you will get greater clarity yourself. So, do tell your dog!

Earlier in the book, I referred to Maslow's 'Hierarchy of Needs'. If you are not familiar with his work, then go look him up on Wikipedia. His research helped him to form the conclusion that everybody needs to have an activity that gives them a sense of contribution, in order to feel self-valued and to be recognised.

There is no better way to do this than to share the 'big picture' of your purpose, vision and values for the business that they are a part of. By inspiring them with your plans to grow the organisation, and what it could mean for them, is hugely empowering. Instead of just 'doing a job', they can see themselves in a far bigger context, with huge benefit to them as the company goals are progressively achieved and new opportunities emerge as a result. Now, this should be incredibly exciting to everyone in the company.

It may have been the case in the past that people just clocked in, did a day's work and clocked out with no real engagement or even interest in the company as a whole, but we have come a long way from the days of the 'dark satanic mills'.

Today things are very different. People want to feel part of something bigger, they want to feel aligned to some purpose, they want to feel like they're useful. Sharing the page with them for the first time can therefore be very powerful.

How to share 'the Page'

When you share the page, it does need to cascade from the top downwards. There are wonderful examples, particularly in the world of retail when it was thought that by just changing the attitude and behaviour of the staff at the sharp end of the business, a business could be turned round, without the directors or managers being involved at all. It never worked! You can't have two cultures running side by side in any organisation.

Either everybody is on the page, or they are not. It can only start at the top at director level, then down to senior management, and down to departmental heads, and so forth.

This gives you the opportunity to make it personal and relevant to them, and for them to ask questions that relate to their areas of responsibility.

When you introduce the page, do so from the left hand side to the right.

Start by talking about what you stand for, and the very purpose of the business. Share with them the ultimate vision of who you are as a business or organisation and what it is that you are trying to create.

Then move on to the values, the expectations we have of each other and how we express that in the way we behave. What is acceptable, and what is not, and how we should support each other in the process.

Share the unique selling proposition of the business and how that makes you different. Talk about the market space you operate in and the promise we're going to deliver to our customers. Don't rush this. It is too important.

Having explained the way you see the business and how you want it to be seen in the marketplace, then move on to your strategy of how you will get there.

Explain the long-term strategy and the key components for each of the departments, the medium-term strategy in the year, and then the short-term actions. This is what you need to do this month and who's responsible for those key actions.

Explain also the Business Growth Indicators and describe the way that they will be measured on a monthly basis.

Now, all of this is really powerful stuff, but equally powerful is the fact that you are sharing it with them. You are showing them great respect by letting them 'inside' the company. They are not just 'workers', but trusted and appreciated colleagues. You are demonstrating that this is not a 'them and us' business, but that you are all in it together. This is not just empty words or corporate spin, but something very real that they can see, touch. You are giving them the opportunity to engage with and be a meaningful part of the business moving forward. Very empowering.

As a result of all this, they should fully understand, probably for the first time, not just what it is their company is all about and what it delivers, but also what it stands for.

They will also understand how their contribution plays a vital role in helping the company achieve its goals, and what that means to them in terms of their future, their security and their own future prospects. It gives them a great reason to want to be 'on the bus' rather than waiting for it to arrive!

An important part of this process is to encourage feedback and input. The best time for this is at the event where you are sharing all of this stuff. Doing this in public makes sure that everyone understands and has the chance to ask questions and challenge you to share your passion and vision. Take time to make sure they all 'get it'; some might take a little longer than others

There is always one!

Inevitably, the law of averages states that not everyone will share your vision. There will always be someone who sits at the back of the room and who is plainly not only on a different page, but in a different book altogether! Sharing your vision with the team and getting them all on your page is vital for your business. You cannot afford to have two separate factions running within your company pulling against each other. At the end of the day, it is your bat and your ball, and you decide who comes out to play.

I know how dangerous a negative influence can be in an organisation. It only takes one cynic who knows the price of everything, but the value of nothing, to undermine your efforts and be a rallying point for discontent. Dealing with that is never easy, but deal with it you must.

It may be that you have inherited some staff from a previous merger or past incarnation of the company and it wasn't possible to deal with this before now, but

if you have a disruptive or negative person on board, simply containing them and countering the effect they are having on everyone else is going to sap energy.

If you have yet to address this issue, then you need to toughen up and face it. It absolutely needs to be one of the actions on your page. You can only achieve your big goals with the right people around you and no hostages!

As a leader, we need to lead through good times, and bad. I don't like getting rid of people but I've had to fire my fair share over the years. It never gets easier, but I always know that I'm doing it for the right reasons

At the end of the day, if somebody is not happy and makes no secret of the fact, then it is in their interests as much as yours to help them find an opportunity that is better suited to their needs.

Also from the company's point of views, an internal terrorist can bring the entire energy of the whole company down, not just the individual leader themselves.

So, by getting rid of a bad apple in the company, you can actually positively affect the morale of the entire company by doing so and create a legend by doing so, but more on this in a later chapter.

Alignment in Action

In launching the Page to every layer of management and all the employees in that business, never forget the power of sharing aspects of it with other stakeholders, partners, associates, investors, and even customers. Any organisation who is really clear of who they are, what they stand for, what their core objectives are and who they serve, will be admired and respected. It can be hugely reassuring to customers to deal with a business that they too can feel aligned to.

As far as internally within the company is concerned, the first stage is to get everybody aligned to the vision and purpose, and for them to have clarity in their role of delivering it.

The next stage is to use the page as part of your recruitment process. You can start to test this at CV stage or application stage. If you look at most of the major corporations, when they're asking applications to be filled in, most of these are values based in parts.

If they get through that, then you would continue in the same way at a face-to-face interview where you would weave in values based questions into your interview techniques. You might also use psychometric evaluation tools, as these have proved to be very effective. You cannot afford to hire the wrong person.

When you get to the final stages of interviews, you can share more of the left hand side of the page with them to help them to buy into the philosophy of the company and see for themselves whether they are a match or not.

Once you've finally got the person that you think you want to recruit in front of you, that's the point when you bring out the rest of the page. This is not something you would do earlier as it is quite a confidential document. However, if by now you potentially have your new operations manager sitting in front of you, it is a great opportunity to share your vision and the big picture that they would be a part of delivering.

You might say, "We think you'll be a fit with us, and also that we will be a fit with you. I now want to share with you what the grand plan for this company is and our core strategy." At that point, you would bring out the full page and share it with them in the same way that you did with your current team. If they are not excited, wowed and just waiting to bite your hand off to start working at the company, you've probably about to recruit the wrong person. So, watch their reactions very carefully.

It's a fantastic final test to just see how people are aligned and if they are bought into the purpose and vision. Because if they're not bought into it at that point of interview, I guarantee they won't be bought into it when they start in your company.

Be warned. It's just like getting married. You only have one chance to get this right!

Case Study

I once worked with a large telecoms company who have created a separate page for each of their divisions. They have one overall page for their telecoms business, but because it is part of a wider group, there was a group page above that.

Below the main page for the telecoms business, there's several other pages. The sales division has its own page, and so does the marketing division and also operations.

The point is that the main page we have been creating is that it is what holds the whole company accountable, including the diversity in all the different divisions. The page is a blend of operations, sales, marketing, HR and finance. But if you need to go down to the next level, there's no stopping you actually having a page specifically for each of the divisions, as was the case with the telecoms company.

Now, the beautiful thing about creating divisional pages is that most of the work is already done for you.

The left hand side of the page hardly changes. Your purpose, vision, values, USP, market space and promise all remain the same.

It is possible, however, that you might want to describe the purpose of that division, as it is a macro business in its own right. This could also slightly change your description of your vision as well, to give it a departmental focus.

If you're doing a strategy for a financial unit of the business, then the focus would be different again. For example, the branding piece would not be so relevant. However, you might want to describe a very specific vision for that department whilst that aligns it with the rest of the company.

On your main page for the company as a whole, you then break down into the subcomponents of strategy, to make it totally divisionally related.

So, within marketing there will be all the various themes of marketing spreading through the page. For your strategies and key actions, you may have a PR element, online element, offline element, branding development, advertising and social media.

By the time you get to the pages for the divisions, rather than referring to the headings as Business Growth Indicators, you'll probably call them Key Performance Indicators. They are not about the business as a whole, but rather the activities of that division.

Earlier on we were speaking about Return on Investment in relation to your marketing. This is the place where you would monitor those figures and also plot the trends using the 'traffic light' system we covered earlier.

You may be measuring trends in social media, online traffic and visitor statistics, pay-per-click traffic and conversions, whatever it may be.

This simple system helps you to keep track of it and to instantly see trends starting to happen. With the one piece of paper, you are in complete control of your division.

Back to the telecoms company I was referring to earlier. They have a main company to manage the group, a separate telecoms arm, a call centre's arm and a new technology arm. When I first started working with them, they were all operating under one banner, but it became apparent that the strategies for each part of the business were incredibly different. It was not practical to try and squeeze everything onto one page so we created the individual pages for each division Now these guys have taken it even further.

In the telecoms company, every individual manager has their own page. This has proved to be a massively powerful way of using the page within their business.

.

Key Points

- Have your own Page as a leader, as big change always happens from the top down in a company

- All systems need to be aligned to the page, like CRM, P&L, operational efficiency etc.

- Introduce the Page to all of your team through annual meet- ings, workshops or smaller man- agement meetings

- Keep a look out for those who are not on board… there's nor-- mally one!

- Use the page to run staff appraisals

- Each department of the company can have individual pages under the main umbrella one

"And some things that should not have been forgotten were lost. History became legend. Legend became myth."

Chapter Twelve
Theme and Reward

By this stage in your journey, to create your own Strategy on a Page™ you are now in a position that incredibly few business find themselves in. Sad, but true. The result is that you have an unfair advantage over all your competitors, who will most likely never have heard about any of this stuff. With what you now know, and with what you are now able to measure and influence every day in your business, just think what a difference it would make to the economy as a whole if every business did the same. In the meantime, make the most of it!

To recap, you now have your completed page, or pages if you have different divisions. You are executing the Key Actions and you are measuring and reviewing your Business Growth Indicators. You have focused on aligning everyone in the company to the page and you're keeping a close eye on creating Legend every day, every week and every month with your employees.

Now you move on to Theme and Reward, which can have a surprisingly positive effect on everyone in business. Once you have alignment across the company and all the elements of the page are well bedded into your company culture and once you are achieving your BGIs every month, it is important that you introduce some element of reward. This is a way of demonstrating that you appreciate what they are doing and that you are prepared to introduce an element of fun as a way of showing this.

Does fun have a place in business? I believe it does. Of course, you must take what you do very seriously. However, those businesses that don't take themselves too seriously tend to have a happier and more positive working environments. Adding Theme is a way of showing this which, when done well, has the effect of energising everybody and giving them a great incentive for moving up a gear. And it really works!

If you are in business, you are in Show Business

Putting Theme into the business

What do we mean by Theme? It can manifest itself in many different ways, depending on what is appropriate in an organisation. For example, an organisation with a dynamic sales force might use Theme more theatrically as part of a competition to drive up the activity necessary to increase the number of sales presentations.

Theme might well manifest itself very differently in a law or accountancy firm when that style would clash with their corporate culture and be inappropriate.

Theme is a way of influencing the way people feel about what they are doing, and giving them an enjoyable and rewarding incentive to do more.

Bringing Theme alive

In some telesales departments, there is a phenomenon known as the 'Rah Rah Day' where theme and reward is used to add an element of fun and competitiveness with prizes for top achievers.

I have seen some sales led organisations run a three month long competition to boost sales during a traditionally quiet time of the year using themes such a 'The Gold Rush'. One particularly impressive competition was on a Bond theme called 'Nobody does it better' with the top achievers being taken to an awards event in Pinewood Studios, where they met some of the actors and stuntmen. A great incentive to sell more, using a theme to add an element of fun.

The important thing is to make a Theme relevant to your people and your organisation. For example, a great story I witnessed was set to a theme of going to battle. The company was in a very competitive environment and they wanted to have quite an aggressive strategy to penetrate the marketplace.

To bring this theme alive, they held their sales conference in the Tower of London and the directors all came in dressed as knights with swords and shields, saying that they were leading the charge and leading the battle from the front.

They then cascaded this theme out to the rest of the company and used it in their company magazine, in their offices and at all their other events and meetings. There were shields around the office with a key legend that they were setting in that time. They also set awards based around the topical theme of knights and castles, and they offered their top achievers weekend retreats in a castle of their choosing. A powerful and very effective use of theme.

Another company was trying to achieve very rapid growth over the next three quarters and they needed to find a way to bring the whole company behind it. In this instance, they chose a space theme, "Reach for the Stars". So, to bring this alive, they created theme posters to display in their offices with key messages about the promotion illustrated with powerful NASA imagery. The key is to make this totally appropriate for your environment.

Now, creative companies, and where you have a young workforce, can really can go nuts with this. But if you're a little bit more staid as an organisation, going over the top could actually act as a negative. However, a competition themed on golf, with a leader board for top achievers, and a prize of a VIP day at the Ryder Cup, might be a real incentive. Certainly you really need to choose the theme very carefully, but equally you need to use it to push the boundaries out by making it exciting and relevant, topical and fun!

Within my own companies, particularly within Business Growth International, because of my particular interest in the extreme sports of mountaineering, desert marathons and Iron Man challenges, I will often use themes around inspired adventure, as this resonates with my passion. But it's important that everybody else is engaged too in their own way. To do this, you can also set individual themes for teams and groups within the business that are relevant and personal to them and their own page.

Some organisations will set yearly themes, as they seem to be the most potent and powerful for them. The challenge, in this instance, is to keep the theme alive, relevant and effective over that long period of time. Without being constantly refreshed and made topical, a theme can lose its effectiveness. When you select your theme, therefore, always choose one that has sufficient layers or facets that will enable you to use it in a variety of ways over your chosen duration.

Other organisations use a Theme for a shorter period to incentivise activity during a slack period, or to kick start a new season.

Equally, you can use a topical theme to reinforce an aspect of values or company promise over a month.

The theme moving forwards for BGI is going to be ultra endurance. We already have plans for completing six marathons back-to-back across the South American rainforest, so that is going to be the key theme for me

Every quarter, when I hit certain results, I'll reward myself accordingly, and more on that in a second.

You can integrate a theme into your page to personalise it and bring it even further alive. Some people will put a theme background behind their page, add logos, photos, or other inspirational elements. It's down to you and how creative you want to be. But the key is to make it exciting, and make it memorable.

Of course, I believe that if you created your page properly in the first place and you are using it to achieve significant things in your business, on a daily basis, and that you have absolute passion for the purpose vision and values that you stand for, then to add anything further would be gilding the lily. But this is personal to you and what helps you to tick, so do what is necessary to make it exciting and a catalyst for achievement.

Whatever your theme may be, whether it's space, sport, ballet, zen, adventure, or whatever it may be, make it yours, make it exciting, make it relevant to your company and use it to bring it alive every single day.

"Leadership is the ability to get extraordinary achievement from ordinary people."

Brian Tracy

Using Rewards

As long as we have a theme embedded throughout the page and throughout the company, we can now use this as a benchmark to reward both our staff and ourselves as leaders, something that is often neglected! After all, you are working the hardest of them all! Therefore, when we set the theme, we must also look at setting individual rewards.

As far as the leader of the business is concerned, we often leave ourselves out of the reward structure and wait until the end of the year to receive a bonus based on profitability or dividends. This is all very well, but probably not motivating enough to bring us to work with a spring in our step on a wet November morning.

However, all of us appreciate being rewarded for stretching that bit further and for doing a good job, so why not give yourself an incentive as well, based on your performance rather than on a whim?

In our debt-ridden society, we have developed the habit of getting what we want when we want it, even if that means borrowing money to do it. If you're sitting there as a managing director of a company, or a CEO of a company or a leader, money might be tight, but you can still afford to buy that TV set when you don't really need to, buy another iPad, or another mobile phone.

We buy all these little treats along the way just because we can, and miss the opportunity to link them to performance.

As our society is fast waking up to the folly of buy-on-demand and notching up easy credit, there is a really good case for getting back to good old basics. If you perform, you get rewarded. If you don't perform, you don't.

Not unreasonable! If that feels a little bit uncomfortable for some of you, then that's good, because it is meant to.

If you are already holding yourself accountable on the page, you have already put in place a robust system with which will identify when all of your BGIs have been met and you are on track. Use it to give you a little reward; after all, you will have earned it!

Conversely, if you are in the habit of regularly rewarding yourself irrespective of how the business is doing, or you may not even know how the business is actually doing, then you are just kidding yourself and you're not holding yourself accountable.

Does this deserve reward? I don't think so! If you are not doing what you should be doing in the company, then you shouldn't be rewarded. This might be tough if you have been in the habit of spoiling yourself just because you can, but as a leader you need to lead from the front and be in total alignment with what you expect of others. You can never have two cultures running at the same time, one for you and one for everyone else. You can't be a leader and not be in alignment.

Case Study

Some time ago, I put this in place within a company I was working in where the owner was quite technically driven and really in to 'big boy's toys'. We put in place a rewards regime where, providing he delivered on next months' performance indicators, he'd get his next iPad upgrade, and if he didn't, he wouldn't.

Interestingly, the next month, when he came along, he was very sheepish and had a pained look on his face. It turned out that he hadn't hit his Business Growth Indicators for the month and hadn't done what he said he was going to do. As a result of it, he hadn't bought the new iPad he was so looking forward to owning. This was quite painful because he really, really wanted it. It didn't matter that he could easily afford to buy it, but he totally bought into the culture of only rewarding when it was deserved and he knew he didn't deserve it.

What a powerful message that will give to his other managers and his staff, who will undoubtedly get to hear about it. He is very much leading from the front and setting legend with it..

Tony Wilson is my mentor from Lifestyle Architecture and he also talks about goals and rewards. We have become so used to instant gratification and rewarding our whims just because we can. Now, Tony talks about this in a different way. He talks aboutAn old mentor of mine used to frame goals not being about what we want, but about what we deserve.

In the world of sport and adventure, there are few hiding places. Even fewer in the Sahara Desert during the Marathon de Sables. Having completed some of the toughest challenges on this earth, I know there is no alternative other than to put in the hours, do the training, put sufficient time into preparing your kit and also getting into the right frame of mind.

How do we make rewards meaningful and effective?

There are no shortcuts. There is no wiggle room, and no way you can bluff your way through.

With something like the Marathon des Sables, if you do put in all of the necessary preparation and survive this gruelling challenge, you will richly deserve whatever reward you have promised yourself for this achievement. It also puts many lesser challenges into their proper context.

Very often, when we think about some of the things we would like to have, we come up with a list of wants, such as trivial high-tech gadgets and expensive indulgences. However, when you do achieve something of real note that you had to stretch for, you quickly realise that these are shallow and meaningless in comparison. You begin to appreciate the true value of real achievement and that the best rewards don't always run on batteries.

Let us assume, as an example, that your long-term strategy covers a period of three or four years, your medium-term is one year and your short-term goals are over one month. Based on that, we should be weaving rewards in on a yearly, quarterly and monthly basis.

Therefore, if we had set our business growth indicators at the beginning of the year and we hit them, that should logically be a reward point.

Now, business growth indicators should be covering all elements of the company. The profitability should be far more predictable as a result of it so it is possible to quantify the amount that you can allocate towards whatever that reward should be.

One of my goals for the year is to participate in the Jungle Marathon. I can understand that this might not appeal to you, but for me it offers a real chance to test myself in a very challenging environment.

For me to do this, I know that there is very clear costs associated with it, so I will need to absolutely deliver on my own BGIs over the next two quarters in order to earn that reward within the company. Believe me, I am highly motivated!

Now, in the meantime, I will also set quarterly objectives to ensure that I stay on track to achieve this big goal. Each of these is based on performance and measured by my BGIs. When I achieve my targets at the end of the quarter, it will allow me to reward myself by taking part in the Original Mountain Marathon, which is a local marathon in the UK and a real test of teamwork, self-reliance, endurance, and navigation skills. This has been a dream of mine for some time, so achieving my quarterly goal will make it possible for me to do it.

At the same time, I will know that I am on track for the bigger goal at the end of the year.

In the meantime, each single month I also reward myself, but with much smaller things and pick them out one-by-one. By only rewarding myself when it is deserved, I stay in alignment and also give an example to everyone in the business.

As I know I will need a number of items of kit in order to take part in these events, I have disciplined myself to only buy them if I perform in the month. If I don't perform, I don't buy the kit, simple as that.

Simultaneously, providing I deliver on the actions that I'm saying I'm going to do, I'll reward myself with longer and longer runs, or endurance runs and weekends to focus in on the endurance work. So, as you can see, I have now created for myself multiple points of motivation.

Pain and Pleasure

Tony Robbins talks about pain and pleasure as being the ultimate motivators for individuals, and I fully agree with him. What we're doing here by using the page as the basis for putting in a reward structure, is that we are covering all bases around the pain and pleasure spectrum.

That is also the case when we look at the purpose and the vision of the companies, because ultimately we are building the long-term pleasure of achieving them. The real power of using the page is when it helps to achieve really big goals, and all the rewards associated with them.

In earlier chapters, we talked about using the page to plan for exiting the company at some point in the future. If you see this as a reward for achieving your page, then you can use the pain associated with not achieving it as a motivation.

What would it feel like if, at the time you had planned to exit the company, you hadn't achieved what you needed to make it possible?

"The secret of success is learning how to use pain and pleasure instead of having pain and pleasure use you.
If you do that, you're in control of your life. If you don't, life controls you."

Tony Robbins

Performance Based Rewards

What would it feel like if you didn't execute on the strategy and realise the purpose and vision that you've tried to create?

With that in mind, now look at the present and apply that same pleasure and pain to the short-term by putting in accountability. Tracking trends on a monthly basis using the traffic light system we described earlier in the book and flagging them up with red, amber and green, lets you know instantly whether you are moving towards or away from those really important
long-term goals. If the pain of not achieving them is big enough, it will be sufficient motivation to force you to do what you know you should be doing, but you're not doing.

Now when you weave into this theme and reward, you are then being rewarded instantaneously. Pleasure, not pain. You are not waiting for the end of the year, as so many business owners do, to get rewarded; you have created a structure in which you are incentivised

by small rewards every single month that you richly deserve, because you've done a good job.

Doing this links together short-term and long-term pain and pleasure, and provides powerful motivation to keep you on track as the leader within the company.

Performance Based Rewards are the final piece of this jigsaw in order to get this installed and aligned throughout the whole company.

We've already talked about alignment with the page, and creating legend within the company.

Now, if you've chosen the right theme for yourself as a leader, as well as the whole company, it's about spreading that theme and reward throughout the company. Getting the reward bit right can be very powerful.

Linking reward to performance

When we talked earlier about legend, we used an example of rewarding people on the spot for going that extra mile and for doing those things which demonstrate their commitment to demonstrating the values of the company.

The next way of using reward is to link it to performance. How do we link theme to reward on a monthly, quarterly and yearly basis? Whilst this is easy to do when related to sales, which are easily measurable, how can you use reward across the entire company in areas where achievement is not as easy to quantify?

Firstly, it doesn't matter what size of company you have, because this is about a principle, not about scale. We are not talking about a big and expensive staff incentive programme, as we have already demonstrated. A 'thank you' and little bit of public appreciation for work well done costs nothing, but goes a very long way.

What I am talking about here is the principle of using the page to measure the monthly, quarterly and yearly performance against the goals that were set, and using a positive result as a reason to reward everyone who played a part in that achievement. The key is that reward has to be linked to strategy. Not to do so is a big mistake.

For example, in some businesses, what might have started off as a simple reward event has, over time, become perceived as the norm. Staff might be thinking, for example, "This happens every year, whether we perform or not, so we are entitled to it." The event has now become an expectation and has no link whatsoever to performance.

If you have got yourself into some bad habits in your company, for example, where staff get taken out for drinks, given a Christmas party, taken out for meals or even, heaven forbid, given a bonus, and none of these are based on achievement against a measurable per- formance, they are going to be very hard to extricate yourself from.

Case Study

But, used well, these little treats can be very effective rewards for achieving against the KPIs that you have in place for them. For example, on a quarterly basis, you might decide that you want to reward everyone in the company by taking them out for a meal, if and only if, the targets are met.

If you're a smaller or medium sized company, and you hit a certain result, then it might be pizzas in the office on a Friday lunchtime for hitting the same goal. If they have all played a part in helping the company to massively overachieve on its goals, then you might upgrade that to taking them all out to a Chinese restaurant.

If people know in advance the different rewards on offer, depending on the level of overachievement, that can galvanise people in extraordinary ways. If these rewards are always linked to achieving your strategy, then everyone, including the company itself, will be a real winner.

A company I worked with in the past had exactly this problem. Some years ago, they had put in place a bonus scheme which rewarded everybody at different intervals. However, when they put this in place, it was not linked to individual performance.

The result was that, for no good reason, people would receive a bonus every quarter, irrespective of what the company was achieving or indeed whether they were delivering what was expected of them or not. The company had really boxed themselves into a corner.

When I became involved with them, the company was struggling and profits were down. As a result, the bonus was not really affordable. But, they had a dilemma. What would happen if they took the bonus away? How would it affect morale? Could staff claim that it was their right to receive it? In effect, the company had lost control and the bonus was now an expectation and worse of all, it was not achieving anything positive for the business. A harsh lesson.

Equity Release

Where a bonus has been put in place and it's not been linked to performance, people will believe they have a right to expect it, even if they don't perform. You could not have a worse culture in any organisation.

Maybe you've been looking for a way to put a performance-based structure in place but you didn't know how to measure it. Well, now you have the page to provide that structure. It can be used in many different ways from performance-based reporting, all the way up to equity release. In this instance, if you have identified the business growth indicators for the year, quarter and month, and they are achieved, then this could be used to trigger an equity release.

Never be tempted to give up equity to senior people in your company without this being linked to performance. Not to do so is criminal.

You should never give up a percentage of your company unless someone deserves it. You only know if this is the case if they have performed consistently over a period of time against the criteria set out on your page.

And finally,

Theme and reward, layered on top of everything else we have covered so far in the book, can really bring your page alive and galvanise everyone in the company to want to help you achieve your strategy.

Make the theme exciting, make it relevant and bring the page alive with it. Once you have your theme set, think about your monthly, weekly, quarterly meetings and theme them accordingly. Have fun with it. Dress up, if it's appropriate, and just bring the strategy alive through that theme.

Then layer your reward structure, firstly for yourself as a leader. So many business leaders fail to include themselves in reward programmes, when they are absolutely the persons that would benefit from them.

We do need to reward ourselves constantly if we are doing what we say we're going to do. But equally, we need to hold off on those rewards, and all those big boy's toys when we don't deserve them and if we're not delivering on what we say we're going to do.
Finally, look to weave the rewards through the company at all the different levels.

Look at opportunities to reward yearly, quarterly and monthly, so that you are constantly keeping everyone motivated and driving forward to meet their KPI and the goals that you have in place.

Look for opportunities to recognise those people who do what they say they're going to do when they say they're going to do it.

And at the same time, bear in mind that some people are motivated by reverse psychology, so use negative incentives if they don't meet their targets.

People need to be very clear on the rewards for doing, and the penalties for not doing. That's how you set your legend through your company and that's how you bring it alive through using themes.

Get this chapter right, and you will really see the magic happen!

Finally, look to weave the rewards through the company at all the different levels.

Look at opportunities to reward yearly, quarterly and monthly, so that you are constantly keeping everyone motivated and driving forward to meet their KPI and the goals that you have in place.

Look for opportunities to recognise those people who do what they say they're going to do when they say they're going to do it. And at the same time, bear in mind that some people are motivated by reverse psychology, so use negative incentives if they don't meet their targets.

People need to be very clear on the rewards for doing, and the penalties for not doing. That's how you set your legend through your company and that's how you bring it alive through using themes.

Key Points

- Reward is a great way of showing your team how much you appreciate them
- Creating a theme within the business culture is a wonderful way of introducing fun to the workplace whilst remaining professional

- Themes and rewards can be in various forms - competitions, parties, hobbies and interests

- Remember to reward yourself! But always link it to performance

Bring your page Alive!

Rhythm is something you either have or don't have, but when you have it, you have it all over.

Elvis Presley

Chapter Thirteen

Rhythm and Pulse

Now we come to the final element to help you get the most out of your Strategy on a Page™, Pulse and Rhythm, to add to your bulging strategy tool box. As with so many other things, timing is everything.

Looking back at the journey we have taken together over the past twelve chapters, you now have in place your page, which has probably been the subject of much revision, and you have gained different insights along the way. You have used it to gain clarity on your purpose, your vision, and your values. You now have a clear picture of what your strategy is and also the business growth indicators for the long-term, medium- term and short-term.

Now, for the purpose of this chapter, I would like you to think of the long-term, medium-term and short-term in terms of one year, one quarter and one month, as this will help us to make the right analogies. These milestones for your strategy already provide you with a 'pulse' for the business.

At the sharp end of that are the critical actions you will be taking on a month-by-month basis, to ensure that you remain on track to achieve your medium- and long-term goals. Experience has shown that a month is a good interval to use when monitoring a business.

248

A week is certainly far too short, and much longer than a month is too long when you need to make in-flight course corrections. Right away, the page has installed a monthly pulse in your business.

At the sharp end of that are the critical actions you will be taking on a month-by-month basis, to ensure that you remain on track to achieve your medium - and long - term goals. Experience has shown that a month is a good interval to use when monitoring a business.

A week is certainly far too short, and much longer than a month is too long when you need to make in-flight course corrections. Right away, the page has installed a monthly pulse in your business.

As a business owner, having that monthly strategic rhythm makes all the difference. But if you really want to excel and to take the business to the next level, you need to be putting in a pulse throughout the company at all levels. That is what we will cover in this chapter. Getting everyone in step.

With your **Strategy on a Page**™, you already have your strategic pulse at the high level in the business. This is driven through the business growth indicators, which definitely drive a pulse of their own. What needs to happen on a monthly basis?

Monthly has proven itself to be one of the best strategic rhythms in a business sufficient, as it usually takes four weeks to obtain meaningful trends and measurements. More than that and it can become detrimental to the company ie. measuring too often, although in some businesses and in some circumstances this can be relevant.

You can also find pulse in the sales pipeline. This is something that definitely needs to be reviewed on a very regular basis to see what new business is coming in and also what is changing. This is one area that benefits from being looked at on a daily, weekly or monthly basis.

Certainly for something as business critical as the flow of new business, this needs to be checked at a minimum of once a month. However, the sales department may well be reviewing this on a weekly basis.

Case Study

During a past recession, I was the commercial director for Northern Europe and Russia for a large multi national company. When the recession really started to bite, the sales pipeline became very, very important within the organisation.

Rather than having the typical monthly meetings and the monthly rhythms, the pipeline meetings came down to every week on a Monday morning. At that time, all the commercial directors would get together and review exactly where all the deals were on a week- by-week basis.

Why? Because every deal counted and depended on how we filled the factory in Poland, and whether people would lose their jobs or not. It was our duty to have our fingers on the pulse, to protect as many people as possible. The influence of the recession forced us to put some very good basic core business principles in place, which helped to get us through and out the other side.

Numbers obviously have a pulse, but everything through the company has a pulse of its own as well if you look deeply enough. So, let's have a think about other pulses, which will vary depending on the size of the business.

At board level, for example, there will be a strategic pulse centred around the monthly board meeting. Now, depending on the size of your business, that rhythm of a regular once a month check on strategy, checking the BGIs and looking at trends, might be sufficient.

There is a good reason why the page has timelines set into it, because when we measure our progress on a month-by-month basis, we can quickly see how easy it is to underestimate the time that things take to happen, and to overestimate what we can do in that same period.

However, by using the monthly pulse of the BGIs, you will know exactly where you are and be able to compensate for anything that is lagging behind.

Strategy meetings should always be quick and punchy and to the point. These are not tactical meetings which may well need to go into some detail and have a broad agenda. Your regular strategy meeting is there to inspect what you expect and to review the BGIs and the key actions, and also to look at the red, yellow and green traffic light coding on your trends. Anything that doesn't relate to the page should be discussed elsewhere and have a different pulse or rhythm.

This is a big mistake that I often see within companies. What is described as a strategy meeting typically turns into a tactical fest where everyone gets to throw their opinion on the table. It seems to be the occasion for the minutia of day-to-day jobs, and minor stuff or minor issues are given major time.

The result is that you end up walking away with a massive to-do list for everyone of tactical issues and you never actually get to strategy. And that is not the point of the meetings. Remember, strategy is major!

In a number of the companies that work inside, I will often chair the board meetings for them. I sit there as an independent and I hold them accountable ensuring that we're talking about strategic, not tactical, stuff. If one of the directors goes off on a tangent into tactical details, I will pull them back because that is for a different meeting.

Orchestrating rhythm across the business

In most organisations, there are a number of key departments such as the marketing department, sales department, operations and finance. Each of those departments will need their own rhythm and it is the role of the managing director or business leader to orchestrate and coordinate it across the company. This is done department by department, meeting by meeting, until the tactical stuff and the strategic stuff are separated in different compartments and different times. It will now be far easier to see rhythm without it being clouded by all the minutiae of everything else.

Separating Tactics from Strategy

Earlier on in my career, I worked with Cable and Wireless in their Partner Services division, at a time when we took on Siemens as a major account, think 8 figure account. I chaired the first meeting which had been called to talk about the strategy surrounding this with the partners involved. Despite this, six hours of valuable time was taken up with tiny details and tactical events.

I vowed this would never be the case again. With the permission of the client, I instigated sub-meetings with all the different departments concerned to take non- strategic issues offline and be dealt with separately. As a result, the next meeting was concluded in an hour and a half with much better energy and a total focus on what needed to be achieved. To do this in your own organisation, you need to do a structure of the organisation in order to understand what rhythms are needed throughout the company. For example, you need a rhythm of the finances going through your company, and understanding of when is the right time each month for you to check them against your BGIs for you to know your numbers.

One department that will have a rhythm of its own is the sales department, which definitely needs to be monitored on at least a monthly basis. In some cases, this might need to be weekly if this information is needed to ensure sales people are on the right track and to enable you to quickly flag up trends.

Now, don't think for a minute that I am advocating a punishing schedule of meetings. Far from it. The rhythm and pulse is orchestrated by you, the leader of the business, in such a way as to provide you with information which you need to know to monitor the implementation of your strategy.

I've done a number of projects as a consultant with a major British plc who always attends meetings in groups of ten. To this day, I still don't know why at least half the people were in the room, probably more!

When you add up the cost to a company of the time of each person attending a meeting, and it exceeds the value of the decisions to be made, then do it by email! If a meeting doesn't need to be held, then it absolutely shouldn't be held.

Only have the people in the room (or zoom) who absolutely need to be there. There needs to be a purpose for the meeting, which is going to be ultimately to add value, add strategic value to the company. The meetings should be quick and punchy

"The hardest job of all is trying to look busy when you are not. That's why meetings are so popular!"

Musical Chairs

There is a whole new trend which recently started in America, which is stand up meetings. The meeting is held in a room with no chairs. As a result, they meet around a table and get the meeting done in vastly less time than it would have taken if everyone got comfortable. I don't see that much happening in the UK yet, but I think the concept is fantastic. Time is indeed money.

Try it for yourself and then work out how much money the company saves in staff time as a result. You might be amazed! Get together, get to the point and then get back on track as quickly as possible so you can drive the business growth.

Got no rhythm?

What if you look around the business and don't see a rhythm or a pulse? What does that mean? It doesn't mean that you are dead, but it might mean that you should be in intensive care! If you are immersed in tactical decisions and are working too much in the business, rather than on the business, you are not running the company, the company is running you. This is where problems can start occurring in the company. There is no pulse.

This can manifest itself in the way communication happens, or doesn't. Communication is a two-way street, from top to bottom and from bottom to top. It is all about providing clear and unambiguous communication from the leader of the business down to every employee.

Coming back up to the leader needs to be clear management information. When there is good two- way communication, everyone has their finger on the pulse.

Taking the pulse across the company

If you take a medical analogy here, if you don't have a pulse in your business, what are you doing? You're flat lining, and if you're flat lining, you're dead as a company. You really do need to think about how you put this pulse through your company.

Let's look in detail at Financial pulse. Your sales pipeline, as we discussed earlier, needs to be reviewed probably weekly by the sales people and by management at least on a monthly basis, tracking what's changed, what's going on and what's going to be different in the pipeline coming up.

Profit and loss, incoming revenues and expenditures should be reviewed on a monthly basis as a minimum.

Cash reserves. In normal circumstances, these should be looked at on a quarterly basis. Depending on how much of an issue it is, cash flow could be done monthly or down to a weekly basis if things are very tight.

In one of the companies I was working with, cash was so tight that they actually got their cash flow down to a daily basis at one point and this enabled them to successfully manage it.

Likewise with your bookkeepers and credit control, they need to have their own rhythms. There will be sub rhythms put in place for tactical reasons, but separate to that, there needs to be a strategic rhythm, probably based around a monthly financial meeting. This is the opportunity you have to look directly at them and understand what they mean, and what they don't.

This is not about just doing meetings and rhythms just for the sake of getting stuff done. This is about giving you the opportunity to step back, look at the numbers, and know that they are accurate so you can make management and leadership decisions moving forward.

Marketing also has a rhythm of its own, which is probably linked to the marketing budget and reviewed monthly.

Rhythm in management

Within the marketing department, there may also be a Public Relations or social media function which could be internal or outsourced to an agency. This too needs to have its own rhythm which can be monitored weekly or monthly. Because of the nature of social-media, keeping a close eye on the numbers being generated might well need to be done on a weekly basis.

Unless social-media is a major part of your business, it's a sub-strategy and should be reviewed as a sub- rhythm, rather than in the boardroom itself. However, you might have a combined total as a BGI and use it on your page to track this activity.

Within your management structure, you will need to have a rhythm with all of the people who report to you directly. There's also a rule of thumb for this, which is that any one person should not have more than six people reporting to them directly.

This isn't set in stone, but if you do have more than seven people reporting to you, you may want to consider putting in sub-management.

For example, if you have six individual reports coming into you each month, you would need at least one meeting a month with each of them, a sub-rhythm to individually to check they're on track, or if there's any issues or concerns.

If you have somebody you work with a lot more closely, either a counterpart or maybe even a business partner, then you may need more regular rhythms.

Rhythm in your management team

For instance, with my executive assistant, who does an awful lot of work for me, we're normally on a weekly rhythm.

However, if we're going through something particularly intense, or there's a lot of change going on in the organisation,

we would move that to a twice weekly rhythm. I'm on a weekly rhythm with my publisher and I'm on a weekly rhythm with my marketing director, because those people are really important to what I'm doing.

With my mentors, I'm also on rhythms with them, which vary between monthly and quarterly. You need to think about all the people that you interact with, especially your clients, and put in rhythms there as well

Clients appreciate regular contact because it demonstrates that you are on their case and that you care. Very few businesses get this right. Put in a regular rhythm with your clients and it will go a long way to making them clients for life.

Although you will be the orchestrator of rhythm in your organisation, you also need to teach your management team to do the same with the staff below them. It is only by doing this that rhythm will become a part of your corporate culture at every level which, along with pulse, is critical for maximising efficiencies and effort.

It is also the only way of ensuring that everybody's aligned to the company and that communication channels are clear, fast and robust.

Of course, you will already have some form of rhythm and pulse going through your company. The question is whether or not it is the right rhythm, appropriate, effective and delivering what you need.

It is natural to be drawn towards tactics and detail, which can quickly eat up your time in countless meetings and leave you

working too much in, rather than on the business. But as the business leader, you need to be able to delegate detail and trust people to deliver.

You remain in charge and on the conductor's rostrum when you put rhythm and pulse throughout the business. You end up with the right information to make the right decisions at the right time.

You can easily tell if rhythm is poor, because there are constantly fall outs or misunderstandings, and information flow up and down the company is so patchy that you are not in a position to make decisions properly based on sound facts. Whichever point you currently are at on that spectrum, now is the time to think this through thoroughly and get the rhythms in place throughout the company.

I once worked with a PR agency helping them to put their Strategy on a Page™ in place. When we started to go through the page and put the rhythms in place, at the very meeting that we were sitting down to discuss it in detail, the CEO came in with the excuse that he had to leave early that day because he had his usual weekly company meeting to attend, which had been scheduled.

He huffed and puffed in front of me, not looking too ecstatic to be going to the meeting at all. So I asked him, as this was the regular company meeting held each week, why was he so stressed about it.

He replied, "The company meeting is just a total waste of time. We just go there, we chat about stuff and we don't really get anything accomplished. But we do it every week, so

it's important that we do it every week because everyone expects it." Now, you can imagine my response to that. If you are of a timid disposition, please look away now!

He was a CEO and had allowed this event to regularly waste several hours of his expensive time every week, not to mention that of his team, for no good purpose! The event had evolved into a tactical fight between departments. No wonder he wasn't looking forward to it, and his staff probably felt the same way! It was just a huge expense, a huge waste of time, with absolutely no result.

Now, in the meeting we were at, we discussed rhythm, the purpose of rhythms etc. and made sure we had a clear purpose for what that meeting was really about.

As a result of that, half of the people who were in the habit of attending didn't need to be there. We then put in sub-rhythms to deal with them.

Based on the obvious power of this, the CEO, to his great credit, acted immediately and instigated a new system based on these principles. He put rhythms in place and over the next few months he diligently applied all the sub-rhythms and put in the various things throughout the company.

The success was phenomenal and the next time we came to talk, you could see the energy in his step and the sparkle in his eye because it was working. Now, the meetings had purpose and they only lasted as long as they should do, they were quick and punchy and all the sub-rhythms were aligned through the company.

In contrast to this, I was working with another organisation, this time a major call centre and technology company. I've been working with these guys a while now and nobody does strategy on a page better than they do. They've been an absolute dream to work with from the beginning and constantly push and test the page to new limits.

Now, when I came on board they had various rhythms through the company, but most of the rhythms were at lower levels. They were amazing at the management level and really engaged with all their staff, looking at the ways to maximise efficiencies and getting alignment at the lower levels of the company.

What they lacked though, was the higher level rhythm because the managing director and the other directors never really got together to have the strategic talks. They were constantly busy with going through the tactical stuff.

Now, when we started layering, because they had already done all the lower level rhythms, it was much easier to now layer in the management side, the leadership side, and the board rhythm on top of it.

With the leaders of the business now sitting down once a month to do that strategic review, it really added both value and much momentum to the company.

I used to chair those meetings because the value of having an independent person chairing them helps to keep them focused on strategy, and not dropping down into tactics.

As you get bigger, the rhythms get more complicated which is why you need the page to help you keep it simple and focused. To ensure you have clear two-way communication right across the business, keep strategy and tactics for separate meetings from the top to the bottom of the company.

Although this will take some time to achieve, I can promise you, once this is put in place, the results are phenomenal. Whatever you are, whatever company size, even if you're a one-man or one-woman band, you need rhythm!

It might be that you need a rhythm just for yourself, with your suppliers or your customers. If you are a small company, this might just mean checking in that once a month.

As you get bigger, the rhythms get more complicated which is why you need the page to help you keep it simple and focused. To ensure you have clear two-way communication right across the business, keep strategy and tactics for separate meetings from the top to the bottom of the company.

Although this will take some time to achieve, I can promise you, once this is put in place, the results are phenomenal. So, I wish you well with your rhythm as we move into the next chapter

---

Key Points

- The milestones you set in your BGIs are the pulse of your company

- Having monthly reviews of these BGIs creates your rhythm.

- All of your suppliers and support team also need rhythm, like bookkeepers, credit control, marketing, management team etc.

"Start with good people, lay out the rules, communicate with your employees, motivate them and reward them.
If you do all those things effectively, you can't miss."

Chapter Fourteen

Conclusion

Well, I have to admit that over all these past 13 chapters, we've been on quite a journey together. If you are reading this page now, it can only mean that you have lasted the distance. There will have been many, I am sorry to say, who will have found this too tough or didn't have the courage to face the difficult questions, which needed to be addressed to move forward through the process.

This was never intended to be a walk in the park, but once you understand the principles and that the process itself is actually very simple to put in place, you are going to put yourself in the top 5% of businesses that really get this stuff. So, I honour you, welcome to the elite business minds, and congratulations!

Way back in the first chapters, we got you to focus on your purpose as a business and why you exist. From there, we looked at your vision of what the ultimate expression of your company looks like and values of what you really stand for and how you behave. Vision, Values and Purpose were the first building blocks of your page. I really hope that the exercises you did in order to get clarity on these three really energised you to move forward to the next section. They are the three core pillars and foundations of any great company.

We then looked at your unique selling proposition, and what

makes you different or special in your marketplace; the market space that you occupy and your all important company promise. It is these three elements of the page which really underpin company strategy.

Being clear on these ensures you maintain a focused approach to the market space, to marketing strategy and execution. In addition, it also ensures that you are focusing on the right space in the right way with the right people, and don't go off chasing shiny pennies needlessly without first considering whether it sits on the page.

S.W.O.T.

I know it seems ages ago when you did it, but we then went off the page and took a look at the Eight Box S.W.O.T. Analysis to understand where you are at right now. This is always a valuable process to do and a quick way of getting clarity. Do keep a copy of your original S.W.O.T. as it will be interesting to look at in six months' time when the results of all your new actions are bearing fruit.

Crossing the line

Having completed all of those boxes on the left hand side of your page, we then crossed that vertical dotted link into the area of strategy itself. We looked at your long-term strategy, medium-term strategy and short- term strategy and the Key Actions which are needed right now

We identified the five elements of strategy that you will be tracking over the short-, medium- and long-term, which should have emerged from the work you did earlier. They would normally be a blend of sales, marketing, operations, finance and HR. There may be other subtle ones, which may be specific to you and your industry, and you and your company. Together, they create a balanced strategy based on all of the core elements of business, not just one, otherwise you are a one trick pony.

Bringing it all alive

Once your strategy was committed to paper, the next stage was to map the business growth indicators, which provide the measurements to ensure that you stay on the right track.

We identified those things that can be measured month in, month out, which represent the company in numeric terms.

The thing about measuring numbers is that there is no hiding place. The numbers are either right or wrong, so we can't kid ourselves. BGIs are the way to get clarity about what's happened in the past, where you are in the present and where those trends will take you in the future.

Based on all of this, you now have the tools to hold yourself to account on a monthly basis to ensure that you do what you say you're going to do, when you say you're going to do it.

Speaking of trends, you also now have that incredibly powerful tool of traffic lighting business trends in colour, and using this as an early warning system, guide your monthly actions and ensure that each core strategy stays on track.

As you will remember, the most powerful and simple way of bringing strategy alive was through legend and instilling the values through the company. We looked at bringing it alive through rhythm and pulse, with you as the leader of your company, putting in the necessary rhythms and orchestrating them throughout the company.

And we finally looked at the theme and reward of how we finally bring it alive by having fun with strategy and rewarding accordingly along the way, based on performance.

So now you can reward yourself!

So, that's it! You have completed the journey and now have your own Strategy on a Page™. You have my permission to feel smug – but not for too long, because now you have to put it all in place.

As you can now see, strategy doesn't need to be complicated, you don't need to spend thousands of pounds on consultants to do it for you, although I highly recommend getting a mentor to guide you and hold you accountable. There are many great ones out there, and here at BGI we pride ourselves at working with the best, so go to the website for more information www.strategyonapage.biz.

It is a simple, yet powerful process that is completely scalable and works for both the largest as well as the smallest of businesses. From seeing countless businesses put this properly in place, the results that have been achieved have been transformational!

The reason this process is so powerful is the thought it causes you to put in to enable you to distil things into the page. It's easy to write reams and reams of stuff of business plans of thinking, but it's in the power of distilling it simply and elegantly. That's where the real power of strategy lies.

Now the doing is down to you. You know everything you need to know to make this stuff work. It will take effort to get everything in place, but after that, your role as the leader will be far easier and much less time- consuming.

Now that so much business is done on the move and out of the office, we have created an extension to the book, which will enable you to be in complete control of your page, wherever you are and whenever it suits you.

The Strategy Software!

The Strategy on a Page™ software is without a doubt an incredibly powerful business tool for when you are on the move and keeps you completely in control when you can't be at your desk. It also makes sure that you stay on top of everything with its topical reminders when things need to be checked or measured. It helps you to hold yourself to account, and kicks you in the ass when you don't.

Now, I realise every business owner is different. This is why, at BGI, we have put a suite of products and tools together to suit everyone

For some people, reading this book will be enough; the light bulbs will go off, the sparks of inspiration will come on and they'll be able to run and use the page in their own way. You can also download an Excel version or pdf at www. strategyonapage.biz

Others will want the software to complement the book, and appreciate being held accountable by technology every month and have it in front of them at all times on their screens. It also has the advantage that it can scale across multiple people in their business using the accountability sections. You'll be amazed how sophisticated and powerful a tool it is!

I do realise that software is not for everyone and having read the book, some of you might have questions about implementation, some will have doubts and others will want to go to the next level.

Therefore, to accommodate everyone's different needs, we have also produced a suite of video tutorials where we go into the various elements in more depth to hopefully give you some different insights.

In addition, we also have our Core programs for you to participate in. Depending on your size Start up, 6 figure, 7 figure or 8 figure we have different programs to serve you. Our core is the Accelerator and SCALEUP programs. See www.BGIstrategy.com and choose the best path for you.

I know that everyone has their own preferred method of ingesting information, so we are also increasing the different ways you can access all this stuff.

For those connoisseurs of business who want to be held accountable and go deeper still, we hold the scale up cohorts. These are for up to fifteen leaders of companies, turning over typically more than a million pounds. It is for those people whose responsibility it is to execute strategy, to discuss strategy and who are prepared to hold themselves accountable both to the facilitation leader and the group as a whole. There is no room for passengers here!

Finally, there's no substitution for having a good mentor and every mentor will have a mentor of their own. Even Bill Gates has a mentor; he is Warren Buffett.

I act as a mentor for a number of companies but unfortunately, I'm full and have a waiting list.

But fortunately, we have many other business growth mentors within BGI who I have worked with and respect hugely, who can guide you in the right direction. Alternatively, seek out a good mentor locally to you. Do make sure they have the right skills set, that they've run their own companies and they understand the space you're in. Understand a mentor is not a coach, it is different, and go online to hear me describe the differences at www.Strategyonapage.biz.

I think you'll find most great mentors have mentors. I practice what I preach - I have three, covering all the different elements of my businesses. I'm not saying I'll stop at four, I'll have as many mentors as I need to help me with the various guises of my business.

What is really important is that your mentor fully understands the Strategy on a Page™ concept so that they can guide you into the difficult questions around it on your journey. When it comes to the complex areas like acquisitions and exit strategies, you will need expert help to guide you.

Strategy on a Page™ has been a long time in development. It has been rigorously road tested in companies of all sizes, and at both ends of the spectrum, and it works! I am passionate about it because I know how powerful a tool it is and how it can make a massive difference to your business.

I've proved it now countless times in many, many companies and the results never cease to amaze me. I've proven it from one-man, one-woman bands, up to multimillion pound companies and the results are always outstanding.

Just keep it simple, keep it accountable, get alignment on it through the company and continually look for ways of bringing it alive.

As you move from theory into putting this into practice, I wish you the success that you will truly deserve. You are part of a very small percentage of businesses that will have an unfair advantage by being 'on the page'. Use it well!

You are the Entrepreneurs of the future and the life blood of the economy. I honour you for stepping up and having the courage to go into business. Now, get on the page, hold yourself accountable and show the world what you can do! God speed.

The End?

The beginning!

"We are what we repeatedly do.
Excellence, then, is not an act
but a habit."
Aristotle